Praise for *Reclair*

"A courageous book and heartfelt story. It's easy to get into a rut and forget your *why* when you're caught in the demands of day-to-day school operations. *Reclaiming Our Calling* will reignite your passion and fan the flame of your teaching and leadership *why*. I can't wait to share the practical resources (e.g., 'Big 3' and 'Let Go' T-chart) with the school leaders I coach."

—**Danny "Sunshine" Bauer**, author and podcast host,
Better Leaders Better Schools

"*Reclaiming Our Calling* is a refreshing read. The stories Brad shares connect our purpose to practice with strategies in each chapter that translate into actions that matter. The reflective nature of this book will give you the chance to consider your own work, and it will provide you a road map to reclaim the passion and purpose that led you to the profession. Be prepared to discover the greatness that is yet to come!"

—**Dr. Sanée Bell**, principal

"Being an educator is the most noble position in the world, but it comes at a cost. Creating systems that will help students learn on a daily basis can drain the life from you. At times, teachers are bombarded with cliché quotes and repetitive sayings as we try to recharge. And to be honest, igniting a passion for teaching is a topic many speakers tip-toe around. Dr. Brad Gustafson stepped up to the plate with this book! He eloquently highlights four types of passion while providing concrete tools for educators and school districts to utilize in order to restore the fire within. This book is a must-have!"

—**Michael Bonner**, second-grade teacher, author, and speaker

"Brad Gustafson is a masterful writer who captures the essence of being an educator through storytelling. *Reclaiming Our Calling* will inspire you to stretch yourself, using essential questions, practical strategies, and relatable stories that connect to 'the core of our calling.'"

—**Dr. Gracie Branch**, executive director, Oklahoma
Association of Elementary School Principals

"*Reclaiming Our Calling* is a gift to all educators. Reading this book will help you reflect on the importance of our why and help you stay grounded in whom you serve."

—**Jessica Cabeen**, national distinguished
principal, author, and speaker

"*Reclaiming Our Calling* is a must-read for all educators, especially those who need a boost of 'Remind me again why I am an educator.' Readers will find this book refreshing, practical, and filled with personal stories that will make you laugh and inspire you to want to keep reading, learning, and re-establishing your passion for our profession."

—**Jimmy Casas**, educator, speaker, author, and leadership coach

"Given the amount of accountability measures, state and national mandates, and negative rhetoric around education these days, *Reclaiming Our Calling* is a message many educators badly need right now. Brad Gustafson uses a variety of character perspectives to remind us why we all entered into the profession."

—**Peter DeWitt**, EdD, author/consultant,
Finding Common Ground blog (*Education Week*)

"*Reclaiming Our Calling* is a rallying cry for everyone who believes educating children is an act of the heart. Brad's Underground Book Club will engage you in an important conversation that needs to be had. It is time for all of us to stand together and proclaim what we already know and believe: School's primary responsibility is to nurture and ignite the human spirit."

—**Christopher Dodge**, principal, The Dexter Park Innovation School

"I am absolutely speechless. This book will create a *boom* in the book world! *Reclaiming Our Calling* starts with a student-written foreword, and the surprising twists just keep coming. It contains a story arc and takeaways that moved my heart and made my brain spin. Now I'm even more inspired to build meaningful relationships with my students. I will be recommending and sharing this book with every educator I know; it's that good."

—**Kory Graham**, elementary innovations teacher

"In *Reclaiming Our Calling*, Brad Gustafson reveals personal stories and anecdotes that get to the heart of our work in education. In this inspiring book, Brad will remind you that the power of an educator is not in the information we share; instead, it is about the relationships we build and creating experiences that unleash genius."

—**Dr. Katie Martin**, head of partnerships, AltSchool and
author of *Learner-Centered Innovation*

"In *Reclaiming Our Calling*, Dr. Brad Gustafson helps educators find their joy and purpose again. Through these powerful classroom stories, reflective-thinking opportunities, and practical strategies, we can reconnect with our passion for teaching and learning and our commitment to the children and families we serve."

—**Donalyn Miller**, author and literacy advocate

"Brad Gustafson is one of those rare human beings who is everything he portrays himself to be through his writing. *Reclaiming Our Calling* is just another example of the innovative ideas Brad shares that I believe can truly revolutionize your school. His heart, the ideas, and the stories just bleed through the pages. I would recommend this book to anyone looking to push themselves further and do what's best for kids (and adults)!"

—**Todd Nesloney**, award-winning principal, author, and speaker

"*Reclaiming Our Calling* contains a common thread woven throughout many heartfelt stories. Intentionally building and nurturing relationships is at the core of the work we do. The exercises in this book will help free you from practices and beliefs that may be preventing your heart from growing. They will help you move away from autopilot mode and give you the freedom to focus on your key priorities. I'd recommend *Reclaiming Our Calling* to all educators who feel like they've lost their way and anyone who wants to rediscover the joy that drew them to this profession."

—**Sandy Otto**, instructional coach and middle school teacher

"*Reclaiming Our Calling* is a practical guide for educators that exudes the passion and commitment that lives in each of us. Teaching is a challenging profession; this book offers leaders, teachers, and parents alike a blueprint for how to develop, improve, and support learning that lasts. Get ready to implement many of these practices in your schools and classrooms tomorrow. You'll wonder why you waited so long to read this book."

—**LaQuita Outlaw**, middle school principal

"Brad Gustafson weaves a tale from his heart that will inspire educators to hold strong to their passion and mission for serving children. His stories are a breath of fresh air grounded in hope, humility, and vulnerability."

—**Dr. Tracy Reimer**, Educational Leadership
program director, Bethel University

"*Reclaiming Our Calling* is grounded in the real work done in schools. Chocked full of personal anecdotes and narrative stories, it speaks to the very heart of why so many of us took up, and continue to work in, education. In a time when gimmicks and so-called best practices seem to be the fad, Brad Gustafson provides a great resource for teachers to get back to the core of great teaching and learning."

—**Josh Stumpenhorst**, teacher, librarian, author, and speaker

"Brad touched my heart and challenged my thinking in this book! He has renewed my passion for reaching each and every one of our students. If we don't know the whole story, we can't help the whole child! This book is revolutionary, actionable, and child centered to the core. Thanks for giving us all hope for a better tomorrow."

—**Salome Thomas-EL**, award-winning principal, author, and speaker

RECLAIMING

OUR CALLING

Hold on to the
HEART,
MIND,
and **HOPE**
of Education

BRAD GUSTAFSON

Published by IMPress, a division of Dave Burgess Consulting, Inc.
ImpressBooks.org
daveburgessconsulting.com
Editing and Interior Design by My Writers' Connection
Cover Design by Genesis Kohler

Library of Congress Control Number: 2018960956
Paperback ISBN: 978-1-948334-04-4
eBook ISBN: 978-1-948334-05-1
First Printing: November 2018

Dedication

To every educator who teaches to the *heart*. You are the hope of our calling. Transformational change is already happening in the spaces you occupy, but you don't need a how-to book to tell you that.

To Mary Burgin, Sue Howard, and Jodi Johnson. You showed me the ropes, but you also showed me so much more. You showed me grace, patience, and possibilities.

To Joey. Through it all, you held true to yourself, and I'm thankful to play a small part in your process of becoming.

BUILD YOUR OWN
BOOK STUDY

1 CONNECT WITH YOUR CREW
- GET TOGETHER WITH A GRADE-LEVEL OR DEPARTMENT TEAM
- START A SCHOOL OR DISTRICT-WIDE STUDY
- OR JOIN THE #UndergroundBookClub

2 CHOOSE YOUR RESOURCES
- DOWNLOADABLE DISCUSSION GUIDE
- STAFF MEETING STARTERS
- VIDEO PROMPTS FROM THE AUTHOR
- CHAPTER-BASED PODCASTS
- QUESTIONS FOR SOCIAL MEDIA SHARING

3 SHARE YOUR LEARNING
- POST COMMENTS, IDEAS, AND QUESTIONS
- HEAR HOW OTHER EDUCATORS ARE #ReclaimingOurCalling

GO TO BradGustafson.com TO GET STARTED

CONTENTS

Before We Begin xiii

Foreword xv

Passion I: The Moral Foundation of Education 1

Prologue: The Four Passions of Our Profession 3

Chapter 1: Higher Ground 15

Chapter 2: Ode to Kenny 35

Chapter 3: Acts of Intentionality 55

Passion II: The Heart of Education 83

Chapter 4: Tattoos and Umbrellas 85

TTTWRNs and Lessons Learned 107

Chapter 5: It Wasn't on My Radar 119

Passion III: The Mind of Education 141

Chapter 6: Autopilot 143

Chapter 7: Find Your Jelly 167

Passion IV: The Hope of Education 191

Chapter 8: Hot Dogs and Hope 193

Epilogue: Loose Ends and Legacy 215

Thank You 231

Notes 235

Let's *Reclaim Our Calling* and Make Meaningful Change
a Reality in Your Organization 247
About the Author 251

Figures

Figure 1.1: Big Three Priorities 33

Figure 2.1: The Core of Our Calling 40

Figure 2.2: Depth vs. Breadth 43

Figure 2.3: Surface-Level Learning Cycle .44

Figure 2.4: Empty Glasses Brainteaser 51

Figure 2.5: Empty Glasses Solution. 54

Figure 3.1: Campground Invention Illustration 58

Figure 3.2: Campground Invention Photograph. 59

Figure 3.3: Reimagining Relationships. 61

Figure 3.4: The Curriculum Tells You "What" 64

Figure 3.5: Mona Lisa Comparison 69

Figure 4.1: Whole Learner Template 94

Figure 4.2: Things I Could Let Go and Embrace 102

Figure 5.1: Staff Lounge Library 126

Figure 5.2: Human Eye Diagram 129

Figure 5.3: Blindspot Experiment 129

Figure 5.4: My Five Radar Items 137

Figure 6.1: Autopilot 151

Figure 6.2: Hexagon 152

Figure 6.3: Rapid Prototyping 153

Figure 6.4: Six Strategies to Short-Circuit Autopilot Thinking 163

Figure 7.1: Talent-Seeking Script 174

Figure 7.2: The Donut Theorem – Find Your Jelly 176

Figure 7.3: Donut Theorem X-ray 178

Figure 7.4: Find Your Jelly 179

Figure 7.5: What Direction Is This Bus Traveling? 183

Figure 7.6: Seeing Strengths—Venn Diagram 185

Figure 7.7: LEGO Book Wall 186

Figure 8.1: Innovative Educators 200

Figure 8.2: Hot Dog Eating Data 203

Figure 8.3: Pole Vault Records 205

Figure 8.4: Taxonomy of Making 210

Before We Begin . . .

Backstory from Dafne (Paolo's Mom)

I grew up in Mexico, and the school system back then had one main goal: Transfer as much information as fast as possible. In the 1980s, the country had a high dropout rate when students moved on from elementary school. Teachers were very busy, and kids were not really encouraged to follow their true passions in the classroom.

Some teachers would even confuse passion with distraction. My brother was victim of that, and his passions were perceived as something negative that needed to get out of the classroom. Luckily for my brother, my mom recognized this and encouraged him to pursue his dreams. It's scary to think about what would have happened to my brother had nobody recognized and supported his talents.

Eventually, I moved to London and worked as an *au pair*. I noticed the school system in England was somewhat different. Kids with talent were *not* seen as a menace, but the school system didn't help either. A student's passions were viewed as neutral, so again, parents were the ones who needed to canalize all this potential. The problem was, the parents of these kids were immersed in the pursuit of their PhDs and didn't always have the time or means to support their children's talents.

I'm now living in the U.S.A. with my own kids, and I have experienced something completely different. This time the school didn't leave me alone, and what they did was explosive! They recognized the talent in my kid. They explored the possibilities. With their resources, they released and fed a little seed in my son.

As Dr. Gustafson describes in this book, this seed has become my son's "jelly." And the jelly is truly contagious. At home, my daughter got inspired by my son. I also saw his passion spread to many of his friends and cousins that are now spending time writing comics of their own. My son is building a community and they are spreading the enthusiasm.

In a society where schools are in the pursuit of integral wellness for children, I hope teachers continue to spark students' passions. The world wants to enjoy the products of their talent. Now I hope you enjoy the words from my son.

Foreword
by Paolo Costea (Student)

Let me start by getting this out of the way. I'm a kid writing the foreword to a book for teachers. Whoa. This is so cool!

Now that I have that out of my system, I want to share a story that starts in kindergarten. This is where I found my true passion.

Like most kindergarteners, I was oblivious and just wanted to play most of the time. (Can you blame me?!) I remember drawing a ghost with big black eyes and showing it to my mom. Naturally, she said she loved it. (I thought it was pretty good for a kindergartener!) Anyway, I started making more of these ghost drawings. The more I made, the more I improved.

My kindergarten teacher, Mrs. Westman, started to notice my drawings too. She introduced me to Mo Willems, and his art inspired me to draw even more. I started designing my own unique characters and creating comic book stories for them. My kindergarten teacher told me I was going to be the next George Lucas. Hearing her say that made me happy, but it also inspired me to keep drawing and writing.

As I got older, my drawing skills continued to improve, and more people took an interest. My classmates would ask me to draw characters for their stories. I even created a book that was placed in the Greenwood Elementary School Media Center. I found out there was a really long waiting list to check it out. (How cool is that?) My art teacher, Mrs. Joselyn, would always say, **"Your art is amazing!"** The people who noticed my work were very motivating to me.

I'll never forget the day my fourth-grade teacher, Mr. McAuliff, made a special announcement in class. He told us a children's book author, Phil Bildner, was coming to our school, and *one* student from every class would be selected to eat lunch with the author. I admit I was only half listening because I was in the middle of another one of my drawings, but I literally dropped my pencil when my teacher announced who the winner was. It was me! Whoa.

When the day of the author visit came, I heard something during Phil's presentation in the gym that I think we should all be mindful of. He said, **"If you have a goal in life, and you wanna get there, don't procrastinate. Reach for it!"** I have never forgotten Phil's words.

During lunch, I remember Phil asking us questions like *"If you could have ONE superpower, what would it be?"* Think about that for a second. What would you choose?

Here's what I picked: the ability to make people happy. And I think I am pretty good at it. I like to make my friends laugh. This is one reason I love drawing.

After lunch, I got to show Phil one of my comics I had brought along. If you're wondering, the comic was about a hippopotamus named Pubble who saves the world from a bunch of evil marshmallows. (As you can see, I have a vivid imagination.) I gotta say, he was impressed! He gave me his email, and whenever I finish a Pubble comic, I try to send him a copy.

After the author visit, Phil sent me an email that said he was friends with Dav Pilkey (the creator of the Captain Underpants series). I told him that was so cool because, at that time, Dav Pilkey was my favorite author *ever*. I didn't think too much of it, but the story didn't stop there.

A few weeks later during science class, my principal, Dr. Gustafson, and my school librarian, Mrs. Gibbons, came in and gave me a package with signed books from Dav Pilkey along with a letter that said Phil had shown Dav my Pubble comics, and he had complimented my talent! He also said something we all should do: **"Keep going. Do what you love to do."**

I'm pretty sure my teachers were behind a lot of this, but the story isn't over. I continued doing school projects, art competitions, and writing for our school library. I even presented at a School Board meeting. Some of this was super stressful, but my teachers, classmates, and listening to my favorite music helped me persevere.

In fifth grade, my art teacher asked me to make some drawings for an art exhibition, and the principal encouraged me to work on a new comic. That was just a bit stressful, but that's life. The point is, your students need to know this: **If you do what you love to do, and get through stress, you'll get somewhere.** I think people that follow their passion are contagious.

I'm in middle school now, and I haven't stopped doing what I love to do. We should all pursue our passions because maybe that will lead us to find new passions. Maybe I should start writing books like Rick Riordan? Maybe I could be an architect like Antoni Gaudí? Maybe I could even be an artist like Leonardo Da Vinci?!

I want to leave you with a final quote from my favorite artist, Jamie Hewlett: **"I want to do stuff that excites me and is enjoyable."** I also want to leave you with one of my comics.

PASSION

The Moral Foundation of Education

The Four Passions of Our Profession

Backstory

Like two animals that have locked horns, an invisible conflict is playing out in education. When I wrote *Renegade Leadership*, I poured my heart into its pages, but I never named the conflict. This book is different. This book *is* my heart, and it seems only right that the stories that follow address the unseen forces educators are all too aware.

WHEN HAVE YOU FELT CONFLICTED IN YOUR WORK SERVING STUDENTS?

Meet Liz

A passionate victory dance erupted in a corner of the classroom. The ill-timed dance elicited an immediate smile from almost everyone.

On the other side of the room, a flash of torn blue jeans streaked out the door. Those blue jeans belonged to one of my students—who was not smiling—and his jeans were heading straight toward the highway. Instead of facilitating the next game of Fraction BINGO with my math class, I found myself pursuing a student who was doing a pretty good impersonation of a raging gazelle.

As the hum of the highway intensified, I could feel my out-of-shape body bouncing so badly my dress shirt started to untuck itself. Undeterred, I continued sprinting until I was almost within arm's reach. Without warning, the young man took a ninety-degree turn while running at top speed.

You've got to be freaking kidding me, I thought.

Before you judge me for thinking in semi-profane language, I encourage you to chase a highly dysregulated student outside while you're supposed to be *inside* getting observed.

It was clear this student was not concerned with my observation—or oncoming traffic. I needed to end this. I gently lunged for his legs before he reached the road. (I was later informed by a woman named Liz that my "lunge" looked more like a tackle, but I'll circle back to Liz in a second.)

As my speedy friend and I caught our breath together in the grass, I looked over and noticed he was sweating as profusely as I was. For a split second, I rationalized that I might not be in as bad a shape as I had previously thought. My momentary ego boost abruptly ended when I looked back toward school.

Half my students had their faces pressed firmly against our class-room window. From that distance, I couldn't tell if they were confused or frightened. But honestly, that wasn't my biggest concern. It was my observation. The observation Liz was conducting. Without me.

When most people hear the word "observation" they think of an administrator or instructional coach critiquing a teacher. Liz held neither of those titles. She was a parent of a prospective student. The week before, my principal had informed me a parent wanted to observe my class. At the time, the arrangement didn't faze me. Seeing my students' faces pressed against the window, I started to second-guess myself.

As I slowly stood up, I was relieved to see some support from the office had come to join me outside. Back in the classroom, I tried to resume our math review game (minus one student), but I had a sinking feeling. What mattered most in that moment had nothing to do with ratios or equivalent fractions.

I approached Liz and sheepishly tried to convince her (and myself) that most of our math lessons went much more smoothly. What I asked my observer next came as a surprise to both of us. I explained that I needed to have an important conversation with the student who was waiting in the office and asked if she could keep the game going. She understood, and the last thing I heard as I walked out of our classroom was Liz calling fractions aloud as students searched their game boards.

I picked my student up from the office and immediately noticed he was not ready to talk, so we just walked. It took me longer than I care to admit, but I eventually discovered he was being very hard on himself for causing such a scene. That's when I took a risk and joked about changing math class from a full-contact sport to something a little less exhausting. A relieved smile indicated he was ready to work on a plan to fix what had just happened.

In the calmest voice I could muster, I asked him a couple questions, trying to get a better understanding of why he had bolted from the classroom. He shared, and I mostly listened.

When we returned to the room, Liz instinctively dropped the Fraction BINGO facade and stepped aside. As a class, we transitioned to a conversation about winning, losing, and being in tune to how others might be experiencing those things. Students took turns revealing their heart for learning and for one another.

The conversation was going surprisingly well, and my runner even managed to offer a sincere apology; however, my jaw nearly hit the floor when a different student—the one who had performed the over-the-top victory dance—spoke up. With a level of empathy many adults don't display, the student said, "Of course we accept your apology, but I also played a role. In the future, I will be a better sport while playing games; I know how much you wanted to win."

I don't remember much about that fraction lesson, and if I'm being completely honest, my students probably don't either. I *do* remember experiencing firsthand how powerful and important matters of the heart can be. It is through the heart that we teach and reach the mind. I also remember how our faithful observer stuck with us the entire lesson. (And I'm pretty sure she noticed how I was learning alongside my students.)

Liz had been in my classroom that fateful day because she was in the process of selecting a teacher for her son the following school year. I suppose you could say she was "scouting." I'm not sure the practice of parent observations for the purpose of requesting a teacher is all that common, but I was too green to have an opinion about it back then.

Here's the scary part: In that hour-long observation, I am positive Liz evaluated me as a teacher. She probably evaluated my athleticism (or lack thereof) too. The reality is that her judgments were not going to be protected under FERPA or any other data-privacy laws. That tackle I had made outside on the front lawn was going to become public knowledge just like my fraction-calling BINGO skills.

You might be thinking this story is about to morph into parent-bashing, and I assure you this is not the case. In retrospect, I give Liz a lot of credit for taking the time to make an informed request about her son's future teacher. All too often, teacher-requests are based upon factors that have more to do with what a neighbor said about a teacher at a garage sale than actual firsthand experience with that teacher.

Now, here's the thing: There is a profound difference between Liz's observation of me and the judgments people further from our classrooms might be making. It doesn't matter whether we're talking about the media, people serving in politics, or armchair educators. The way they are trying to define our work doesn't always position us to do immense good for the students we serve. It's just the opposite, really. The question is, how do we take back teaching?

More Than a Number

The hour or so Liz spent observing me in (and out of) our classroom showed her only a small fraction of the work educators do. I know math review games are serious stuff, but at a certain point, my students needed something more than Fraction BINGO from me. I had to pause and meet them where they were.

Despite external pressures to raise test scores or self-imposed pressure to facilitate a lesson Liz would value, heart-work was what my students needed from me most during my observation. Does this invisible struggle between academics and student well-being sound familiar?

We know children are more than numbers, so why are so many of us feeling pressure to defer to decisions that will increase scores? I believe our work has to be about much more than a hyper-focus on high-stakes testing. The work we do to elicit empathy and support students' social-emotional learning truly transcends time.

This might be more than we can say for Fraction BINGO, but let me be clear: This is not a book about ignoring accountability. What we need to confront are the destructive testing influences that aren't serving students.

If you're anything like me, you're growing weary of watching assessment data used primarily to label and group learners. Seeing high-stakes testing results reported in newspapers like box scores from a baseball game doesn't feel right either. I have even been part of conversations involving community members who spoke about test results in terms of how their property tax values would be impacted. (I wish I were kidding.)

It's unrealistic to think we can serve two masters.

Prioritizing students' social-emotional development while embracing meaningful assessment practices is possible, but we need to value the learner—the whole learner—above all else. That is the moral foundation of our work, and learning that lasts flows from this overarching priority. We can no longer put a painfully narrow definition of student achievement on a pedestal and hope the whole learner will somehow prevail.

It doesn't work that way.

This is a book to help us think and do differently. It is a book that honors the past while unabashedly embracing the opportunities in front of us. And it is about our collective response to the unhelpful labels being thrust upon us.

The Umbrellas We Carry

We live our "educator lives" in public, with many people making snap judgments about our values and work. The truth of the matter is, being labeled can hurt—even when you're lucky enough to get a good label.

I have been doing bus duty outside each morning for several years now. I call it "bus duty," but the bulk of my time is technically spent assisting parents who are dropping off their children. I love connecting with kids and greeting families. Despite how appealing I've made bus duty sound up to this point, it is not all sunshine and roses.

Being from Minnesota, you'd think my least favorite part of bus duty might be the frigid temperatures during the eight months of winter we have, but you'd be wrong. What I like least about bus duty is actually the rain. There's something about starting the day in wet socks that makes my skin crawl. That's why one particular morning still stands out.

It was raining, and I was "umbrella-less." (A made-up word, I know. And please get used to it.) I searched a storage closet in the main office and grabbed a dusty, old umbrella. When I popped open my newly claimed umbrella, I couldn't help but admire its antique wooden handle. Perhaps it's the craftsman in me, but I always appreciate solid wood construction—even on umbrellas. With renewed hope that I'd remain relatively dry, I headed back outside to greet families like any other day.

After fifteen minutes of helping to open car doors for our youngest customers, our morning drop-off time wound down. That's about the same time a co-worker approached me with a bewildered look in her eyes. I was having a hard time understanding why she appeared so scandalized until she pointed out the giant beer logo that was stretched across my borrowed umbrella. I had been so focused on greeting everyone as they arrived that I totally missed the large alcohol advertisement.

Aside from the fact that I had just violated multiple sections in our student handbook, I was most worried about being labeled. Have you seen the headline about the principal who enforces the student dress code while carrying a beer umbrella? Me neither. I quickly folded up the beer paraphernalia and went inside to take off my jacket. (And in case you are wondering, my jacket was *not* one of those freebies cigarette companies give away to promote their products.)

I'm guessing I'm not the only one trying to avoid being labeled. I don't think any educator wants to be pigeonholed or pressured into being somebody they're not. The work is hard enough as it is. So how do we set down our borrowed umbrellas and hold on to all the things we *do* stand for?

Four Passions

This book is built upon the belief that meaningful change happens when we do two things well: First, we need to hold on to the passions of the whole profession. Second, we need to embrace the moral foundation of teaching. When we do these two things consistently and collectively, we will facilitate learning that lasts. I don't pretend to have all the answers, but I'm confident we can become an unstoppable force for good by dialoguing more about these passions and this type of learning.

In that respect, I hope you'll consider this book part of a larger conversation. You'll notice it is organized into four parts, one for each passion. Here's a quick preview of each of the passions:

Passion I: Moral Foundation

The first part of this book stakes out the moral foundation of teaching. (Although I bet you don't need anyone else telling you why you get out of bed each morning.) We already know doing what's best for kids is an ethical obligation that extends far beyond preparing students to do well on testing day. Learning that truly transcends time often involves skills that are very difficult to measure.

Passion II: Heart

Our very existence is forged from matters of the heart. We are relational beings who thrive when we experience a sense of belonging and connectedness. Ignoring our hardwiring in pursuit of all things measurable provides an incomplete picture of the human condition. We need to start seeing value in our vulnerability while recognizing how relationships support learning that lasts.

Passion III: Mind

The passion of the mind makes learning possible. Curiosity is as precious as gold and capable of fueling a lifetime of questions. (I'm a bona fide nerd and somebody who loves reading every single sign inside museums, so you had to see this coming.) We need to turn off autopilot mode and find new pathways to help students experience content in ways that make their curiosity come alive.

Passion IV: Hope

One of my favorite parts of being an educator is meeting with parents and seeing the twinkle in their eyes when they talk about their children. (Liz positively lit up when she talked about her son.) Even when conversations center on goals for improvement, it's difficult to ignore the hope parents possess. These moments are visceral reminders that nothing compares to the power of hope. Harnessing hope involves tapping into the strengths and talents of everyone in school.

Together these four passions reflect the past, present, and potential of our profession. Heart, mind, and hope are ours to wield on behalf of the whole learner. When we lean into these passions, we tap into our God-given talents. We are called for such a time as this!

Regardless of what brought you to this book, I hope a spirit of simplicity and vulnerability flows from the stories within. I also hope the stories (re)awaken these four essential passions in you. These stories serve as a connective tissue between the work we love and the changes we'd like to see.

You'll also find insights from educators serving in a variety of roles linked to some of the stories. These "Voices from the Field" offer fresh perspective on the joys and challenges associated with our work. At the conclusion of every chapter, you'll find additional resources to support the real work you're doing in pursuit of learning that lasts.

Analogous to Teaching

While recently conducting a workshop for teachers, I invited participants to share one photograph representing their role in education. As teachers sifted through pictures and talked, I sat down and listened to the heartfelt comparisons they drew.

One participant shared an image you might be able to relate with. With a quiver in her voice, she explained how it felt like teachers are being asked to climb up an escalator while the stairway treads are crashing down toward them at an unforgiving pace—the opposite of how an escalator is supposed to function.

The care and concern in her voice resonated with everyone in the room, and I haven't been able to get the image of escalator treads out of my mind. All of this has me thinking: We don't need to ask ourselves to try harder or do more. If I know anything about educators, it's that we would be willing to walk through a wall for our students, never mind leaping up escalator steps coming toward us.

I've continued to reflect on this escalator analogy, and I keep coming back to the importance of standing on a solid foundation—a foundation that supports learning that lasts. This foundation is so much more than numbers. We need to be moving toward a better place for our students, a place that emboldens the heart, mind, and hope of teaching.

In a spirit of togetherness, let's flip the switch to that escalator so it takes us in the direction we know we need to go for the students we serve. Let's defy the labels some would have us wear and show the true potential of our calling.

 #ReclaimingOurCalling

CHAPTER 1

Higher Ground

Backstory

Seeing students as whole learners—lifelong learners—is the *moral foundation of education*. No program or policy that prioritizes short-term gains should ever prevail over learning that lasts. Everything we do connects back to the students we serve.

WHAT MAKES YOUR CLASSROOM OR SCHOOL A PLACE WHERE PEOPLE FEEL SEEN?

Meet Joey Forrest

The problem with a shell is that you're all alone inside it. That was Joey's dilemma. No matter how many life preservers and parachutes the universe threw at him, his shell seemed impenetrable.

The kid couldn't catch a break.

Meeting Joey started out as a form of forced charity. This may sound harsh, but my parents would send me across the street at least once a week to see if he could play. Each time I rang his doorbell, the same routine played out. First, his sandy-blonde hair would bound toward the doorway accompanied by an unparalleled amount of optimism.

Next, I'd shift my weight and focus on the tired brown welcome mat on his front step. Or I'd stare at the planter of bright pink Geraniums next to the mat. Or look at my Reebok Pump shoes. Or anything other than Joey himself.

After that, I'd say, "Want to play?" Watching him twitch and turn as he pleaded with his mom was too much to bear.

But her muffled response always came like clockwork: "Are your chores done?!"

Somewhat deflated, Joey would start to twitch and explain how he needed to paint the house, mow the lawn, or start some other project. He seemed to have accepted his new role as the family handyman ever since his parents had divorced, but his quality time with paint brushes and plungers wasn't doing him any favors when it came to making friends in our neighborhood.

I think most people sensed he was destined for more, or at least destined for different.

Aside from the occasional marching orders across the street from my parents, I probably wouldn't have paid much attention to Joey if it weren't for the fact that he invited me to his birthday party one year. You tend to start noticing other kids when you get invited to their birthday parties. One thing I had started to home in on was his twitching and mini-seizures.

One time in school, I was looking in Joey's direction during a social studies test, and he started flinching. I don't think he caught me staring, but I definitely saw him.

Not that we needed it confirmed, but our teacher eventually did one of those whole-class talks acknowledging Joey had issues. She shared how he struggled with a condition I had never heard of before. It wasn't actually called "mini-seizures," but that's beside the point right now.

As an educator, I know these kinds of whole-class talks are intended to elicit empathy and help a class develop a shared understanding about the challenges a student may be facing. Despite the talk feeling a little forced at the time, I think it actually helped us better relate to Joey. He didn't stop flinching, but we all tried to stop staring. Well, all of us except Kenny Mauer.

Try This!

Try incorporating picture books (or novels) featuring a variety of diverse characters in your class read-alouds. Regardless of your role, read-alouds and the conversations they inspire create a more natural opportunity to have one of those "whole-class talks" that Joey had to experience; additionally, taking the time to read with students of all ages builds relationships.

Meet Kenny Mauer

Kenny Mauer's hair always reminded me of the contours on a classic corvette. This probably had more to do with his dad's choice in vehicles than anything else, but either way, I was a little jealous.

I think most kids were. His freckles were captivating too, but for a different reason.

Kenny's freckles were like dark shards of twisted metal laying on top of a fresh pile of snow. His pale skin seemed to illuminate them. Joey explained it best when he compared the freckles to an anglerfish trying to lure its prey in for a look. We didn't dare say anything to Kenny about his freckles because, as with the angler fish, the moment you got caught staring was the moment you got destroyed.

There was no doubt in our second-grade minds that was exactly what Kenny would do to us.

Kenny was the unholy trinity of class bullies. He was a class clown, genuine jerk, and ninja all rolled into one. And he wasn't the cool kind of ninja in case you are wondering. He stealthily tried to make everyone's life miserable. Especially Joey's.

Slightly larger than almost everyone in our class, Kenny created all sorts of problems for Joey (and anyone who had a mind to stick up for him). Kenny was like a heat-seeking missile who seemed to carry hurt and destruction wherever he went. Once he zeroed in on a target, he'd find a way to strike and then slip away without anyone knowing he was to blame. Bullying on the bus was his specialty, but he wasn't above stealing friends or other forms of manipulation.

Back to Joey

One of the only reprieves for Joey came when he got to leave for his enrichment classes. Although I didn't see what went on in those classes, I know he got to work on special projects and build cool stuff. (At least it looked cooler than the work the rest of us had to do.) Don't get me wrong, I would never have traded places with Joey.

Not in a million years.

As if the mini-seizures (that weren't really mini-seizures) weren't bad enough, he had an even bigger problem. A problem that everyone but Joey seemed to recognize: He couldn't see past his own shell.

Joey's shell made him a walking contradiction. He desperately wanted others to look beyond what was outwardly obvious, but he seemed incapable of opening up long enough to let anyone see inside. By his own sad example, Joey taught me that you're never really out of your shell until the world can see your feathers. Suffice it to say that Joey's journey was definitely more "shell" than feathers.

Of course, I had insight into Joey's home life that many of my classmates didn't have; for example, Joey seemed to grow taller any time his dad would visit. For whatever reason, those visits seemed to make his mini-seizures less noticeable too.

Occasionally I'd peer out our living room window to check out the latest chore or odd job Joey was working on. One day I noticed him grinning from ear to ear. For once he wasn't playing catch by himself. He had traded his hammer for a baseball mitt and was taking pitches from his dad. After only a minute or so, Joey missed one of his dad's pitches and his white T-shirt transformed into a soggy red mess. The kid truly could not catch a break (unless it was a breaking ball to the nose).

I never saw them play catch again. It seemed like his parents' divorce had left a dad-sized hole in Joey's life that even his dad couldn't fill.

Fortunately for Joey, my parents were not the only ones cheering him on. He had teachers in his corner who ensured he was also somebody our class came to love. They made it clear there was a place for him in our school, and we just followed their lead. To be fair to Joey, there were a few things he excelled at (besides swinging a hammer at home). For starters, he was one of the fastest kids in our grade level.

He also did pretty well on most of the tests he took. I'm sure that's why he got to go to those enrichment classes.

Eventually, Joey and I became really good friends, but I'll get to that later. For now, I want us to reflect on the conditions that made school a place where somebody like Joey could thrive. I'm not just talking about academics but the social aspects of school too. Wherever Joey went in our school, people seemed to truly see him even if he didn't see himself yet.

Unfortunately, this is not true for all students.

All of this has me wondering, *What would school look like if we held the whole learner in the same regard as high-stakes test scores?* This is a question I often ask when facilitating a keynote or workshop for educators. It's also a question that has evolved over time, just as my own learning has, but the emphasis is always on seeing and doing what's best for kids—just like Joey.

> ## *What would school look like if we held the whole learner in the same regard as high-stakes test scores?*

Seeing and doing what's best for kids is not always as easy as it sounds. This is because what one educator feels might be best for a student may not align with the philosophy and priorities of another educator; for example, have you ever asked for something from a supervisor or colleague and been disappointed they didn't see the same value in your idea?

Trying to do the right thing for students can sometimes feel like pushing a boulder uphill. I think this is due, in part, to that invisible conflict I mentioned in the prologue. But there's another reason.

Did You Know?

Holding the high ground is a widely recognized tactic in battle. An army holding the high ground benefits from enhanced vision, superior surveillance capabilities, and increased range in weapons. There is an additional advantage that may resonate more with educators. Holding the high ground allows an army to expend less energy than the opposition who is trying to fight uphill.[1] Wouldn't it be great if teaching felt less like running the wrong way up an escalator, and more like gliding down a zipline? When we start from the moral imperative to do what's best for the whole learner, things begin to flow. The obvious challenge is determining what to do when things are *not* flowing.

It's safe to say that teaching will never be easy. As one of my mentors liked to say, "It will be worth it, but it won't be easy." She was right.

Try This!

When you become frustrated with a challenging situation at school, or if something seems harder than it should be, try to identify the unspoken priority. What thing(s) have others prioritized that you're trying to push against? Working together to identify one another's high ground is one of the most meaningful processes you can enter into as a classroom or school community.

Wouldn't it be great if teaching felt less like running the wrong way up an escalator, and more like gliding down a zipline?

Meet Mrs. MacLean

Becoming a teacher is one of those rare times when a person comes face-to-face with their true calling while fully realizing how grossly underprepared they are to do so. I suppose that's the whole point of student teaching though.

Our university teacher-preparation program prided itself on a co-teaching model where student teachers would work side by side with their cooperating teachers. Mrs. MacLean was my cooperating teacher and mentor.

Just like when I first met Joey, I noticed some things about Mrs. Maclean right off the bat: Her eyes were big, bright, and sparkled with curiosity. She was really easy to talk with and even more fun to listen to. The large hoops hanging from her ears would bounce with enthusiasm any time she was telling a story. Her short hair pretty much stayed in the same place no matter how excited her earrings were.

Although she was average height, she seemed really tall. I can't really explain why, it's just the way it was. She was confident, encouraging, and adept at seeing her students as whole learners.

I was less adept. At everything.

One day our class was in the computer lab working on a writing project. Being the astute observer I was, I noticed a hand flailing wildly in the air. I was closer to the hand than Mrs. MacLean, so I darted over to the boy—fully intent on changing the world.

I quickly realized I had no clue about the computer program he was using and knew even less about the curriculum. In short, I felt helpless—yet I was supposed to be doing the helping. I must have experienced a moment of divine intervention just then because I suddenly recalled some advice from one of my university professors. If I recall correctly, I am pretty sure my professor had been talking about how to handle student discipline issues, but I crouched down to try to get eye level with the boy needing help anyway. With my hands propped on my knees, I looked at his workstation and tried to make sense of his questions as best I could.

After a minute of crouching, my new-teacher legs began to burn. I noticed an extra chair in a nearby corner of the computer lab so I slid it over to get more comfortable. Approximately two seconds later my world came crashing in. Literally.

In the very same space where I was trying to prove my teaching acumen, I found myself flat on my back, staring at the computer lab ceiling and wondering, *What just happened?!*

My thoughts quickly shifted from my fall to the curious onlookers around me. Computer labs back then were traditionally quiet places, so there was no escaping the fact that Mrs. MacLean and every single one of our students heard me and my defective chair hit the floor. Hard.

I found my bearings, dusted off my pleated pants, and resumed "helping" the student from a half-crouched position. A few moments later, I felt a gentle tap on my shoulder and turned around to see Mrs. MacLean standing beside me. I stood up so we were shoulder to shoulder, and she whispered something in my ear like only a true mentor could, "You might want to untuck your shirt because your pants split wide open in the back, and everyone can see your underwear."

That was it. Then she walked away. (And who was I to argue with her sage advice?)

Looking back on that disaster, I learned a valuable lesson. Mrs. MacLean taught me early in my career that it's not about me, and it never will be. She didn't tell me to go home and change my pants. She gave me advice on how to make my ripped trousers less of a distraction to our students so we could all get back to work! When we keep teaching, learning, and empowering students to do the same, they will always come out on top. That's our calling.

I have encountered plenty of obstacles, such as not having a clue how to answer a student's questions, throughout my career in education; likewise, I've run into my share of awkward moments, not the least of which was crashing down to a cold, hard computer-lab floor. Holding the high ground *doesn't* make us immune to challenges; it *does* give us the confidence that we're working towards the right priorities amidst challenges.

Obstacles will present themselves in the form of difficult situations, challenging co-workers, and improperly welded chairs. But one thing is true of most of the difficulties we experience: Adversity can always teach us something if we let it. Vulnerability and humility accelerate our learning, but even the smallest excuse or deflection will stunt our growth. In case I wasn't clear, we're no longer talking about a broken chair.

> *Adversity can always teach us something if we let it. Vulnerability and humility accelerate our learning, but even the smallest excuse or deflection will stunt our growth.*

I understand that sometimes it can take a little longer for a person to get to a point where they're ready to change. That's okay. We tend to be slow to change when we've been burned in the past. Other times we resist change because we don't feel valued or safe. Whatever the case may be, we have got to be willing to grow even when doing so feels uncomfortable. The amount we grow in any given challenge is a direct reflection of the amount we're willing to admit we don't already know.

> *The amount we grow in any given challenge is a direct reflection of the amount we're willing to admit we don't already know.*

Most of us would not have chosen to endure the difficulties we've encountered in our classrooms and careers. But when we get through these things (and we will), we have the choice to walk away more equipped to overcome future challenges—or not. And as my dad always said, "Time heals all wounds." There's a lot of truth to that statement. (I would factor the grace of God into this equation, but there's another book already written about that.) Whether we're talking about a good day or downright impossible dilemma, holding firm to the priorities the high ground represents is a daily discipline—as is learning from the challenges we face.

We've All Been There

You might be surprised to learn I made it through my student teaching experience—broken chair and all. After several years of teaching, I eventually took on some additional responsibilities, including serving as our school's Student Council advisor to more than one thousand students. (It was pretty awesome.)

Later I applied for some curriculum-writing time and began developing five-minute mathematical power lessons. The lessons were intended to provide a mathematical boost to students and maximize their growth on a popular, nationally normed assessment. I designed each power lesson based on some sample questions and leveled resources made available by the same company who published the nationally normed assessment.

Creating and watching my students use those power lessons excited me. Seeing them progress through the practice problems made me feel like I was making a difference. After all, they were practicing important math skills correlating to our state standards. My students performed very well on their year-end assessments and exceeded growth targets using multiple metrics over time. Looking back, I realize I had fallen into a trap countless educators have encountered. I now believe my students' performance came at a cost.

I wonder what our classroom might have looked like if I had invested just as much time teaching the whole learner as I did preparing students to perform on one particular test. I had doubled down on short-term gains when we could have also been pursuing learning that lasts.

The tests were required, and I knew my students' achievement mattered, but I could have supported students as whole learners at the same time. It never needed to be the either/or thing I made it out to be. I know now that the moral imperative to teach and reach the whole learner—in a manner conducive to learning that lasts—is the high ground we need to hold on to. Settling for anything less, or prioritizing things in the incorrect order, is a very slippery slope.

Before you think you're immune to systemic pressures or the influence of others advancing an achievement-at-all costs narrative, I have a cautionary tale. We are all susceptible to perceived pressures from colleagues and the culture in which we're working. This applies to teaching to the test, but it also applies to other aspects of education.

This is somewhat embarrassing to admit, but I'll do it anyway: There were times when I was teaching that I actually carried home a "decoy bag" just so my colleagues wouldn't question why I was leaving without papers to correct. There were times I worked past 7 p.m., 8 p.m., and even 10 p.m. at school, but somehow I still felt guilty if I didn't carry a bag full of extra work home.

I recognize I was newer to teaching in my decoy-bag days, and I needed to put more time in to better understand my craft, but that's not my point. We're all influenced by the culture and pressures around us. That's why developing a shared understanding of the high ground is so important. Imagine what would happen if we stopped putting energy into decoy bags and pushing boulders uphill and started caring more about the actual priorities we're called to hold on to.

Our Calling

When I reflect on the reasons I said "yes" to this crazy adventure, a few things come to mind. I said yes because I want to improve opportunities and outcomes for all students. I feel called to create conditions where a learner's preexisting passions are always nurtured. Always.

I said yes because I feel called to collaborate with others to enhance how students experience school. I'm not just talking about making cosmetic improvements either. I believe school should be a place where deep and personal learning is fueled by curiosity and connectedness. The reason I can hardly wait to get up each morning is an internal drive to create conditions that unleash the passionate artist, engineer, leader, reader, inventor, and dreamer inside every learner.

Try This!

Take a moment to reflect on one part of your job that gets you up each morning (or back up after you fall down). Why did you say, "yes" to this profession, and what's your end game? Try writing down your thoughts on the blank pages in the back of this book if it's helpful.

Voices from the Field

"I believe passionately that students deserve intellectual freedom and support for their personal passions. What gets me up in the morning is my opportunity to connect students and teachers with ideas that help them grow (wherever the ideas are found—in books, online, or in human resources) and to support their learning, intellectual, and emotional growth."

—Carolyn Foote,
high school librarian, Texas

I don't pretend to know what any educator's specific calling is. That's between you and somebody way above my pay grade. I am, however, willing to bet you didn't list "Preparing students to do well on standardized tests" as your overarching priority when you became an educator. A student's achievement on a test is an incomplete characterization of what we need to do to facilitate learning that lasts. I think we all instinctively know that. The challenge is living and teaching with this foundational understanding and calling in mind.

Higher Ground

I recently received an email from a parent who was on cloud nine. As I read her words, I could tell she firmly believed her daughter's life had been changed by a teacher in our school. She explained how a unit on innovation, facilitated by one of our grade-level teams, had sparked something special in her daughter, who is now a middle schooler.

The parent went on to share how her daughter had started a fashion business, created a stellar website, and participated in multiple interviews with local media since her time in elementary school. They had even traveled to New York over the Summer to connect with some industry experts.

Some of the fashion details she shared went over my head, but I definitely didn't miss her mentioning how our team took time to cultivate her daughter's passions. They provided her daughter a powerful space to research, refine, explore, and fail. This grateful mother's email served as a powerful reminder of the need to help students achieve at a high level *while* seeing them as whole learners. The high ground is about consistently doing both.

Teaching and leading from the high ground ensures we see value in tested and untested things, such as social-emotional learning, creativity, exercise, and movement in our schools. Teaching the whole learner involves clear content standards and a clear path to student passions. Teaching the whole learner doesn't mean we disregard academic achievement; it just means we refuse to disregard everything else important.

Try This!

Try adding this simple yet powerful practice to some of the assessments, quizzes, or surveys you administer: The next time students take a test, invite them to add one open response item at the end where they share something they'd like you to know. This could be a passion, hobby, picture, or something weighing on their minds. The information you glean from this might turn out to be the most important data you collect all school year.

> *The single greatest tool to optimize a student's options in life is an educator's drive to teach the whole learner.*

When we commit to seeing the whole learner, we regain the high ground, and the work begins to flow. I'm not saying it will be easy. I'm just saying it will be right. The folks out there who would have us hurdle up escalators trying to get students to produce a higher number or designation for their school are misguided at best. If we focus on only one facet of student success, there will be students who never really feel they belong.

All Means ALL

My oldest child has high-functioning autism, so I know all too well the agony students (and parents) experience when they don't feel like they belong. For some students, school is a painful reminder of their deficiencies and differences. For whatever reason, they do not see themselves in their school, or haven't been taught how to tap into their unique strengths.

Experiencing belonging goes beyond cognitive considerations and addressing social-emotional stigmas. Students who have experienced trauma—and those who might even be more difficult to teach as a result—are counting on us to stand by them. Seeing and valuing all students must include intentionality around seeing the strengths brought from cultures other than our own. All learners need unconditional support, and if we're doing it right, this support could look different depending on what a particular student's strengths and needs are.

Voices from the Field

"I am driven each day by my students' expectations of me to inspire, mentor, provide unconditional support, and to protect their learning."

—Jon Zetah,
elementary school
teacher, Minnesota

When we commit to creating schools that see *all* kids, we will understand just how personal learning can be. Reclaiming our calling requires clarity on *who* we're teaching and *why* we're teaching them. It also requires an acknowledgement that the two opposing forces influencing everything in education can actually work in concert with one another. Let's look at *how* this might be done.

The Beautiful Game

Soccer has always been in my blood. (There's a reason many countries refer to soccer as "the beautiful game.") While I was teaching, I had the opportunity to serve as our high school boys' varsity soccer coach. Our team struggled for several years. Our players and coaching staff knew the work we were putting in on the practice field wasn't translating to the win-loss column yet. At the same time, everyone believed we were doing the right work. We were teaching young men to be better sons, brothers, and teammates through a combination of tactics, skill instruction, and character education. We didn't dismay, because we believed the skills we were cultivating in our student athletes would eventually translate to strengthened families and communities.

Our soccer team was about more than the game. We formed an elite club we dubbed the "CIA" which stood for commitment, integrity, and attitude. Our coaching staff and team captains took time to talk about these traits—a lot. We made T-shirts that had huge CIA letters on the back and integrated some character-based recognition into our end-of-year soccer banquets. The hardware we gave away to honor our leading goal scorers and MVPs dwarfed in comparison to how we celebrated our CIA award winners. Through the years, a funny thing started to happen: Our team's balanced approach to coaching soccer skills *and* soft skills translated into more wins on and off the field.

I share this story because this approach can lead to learning that lasts in the classroom too. The moral foundation of teaching is helping the whole learner grow. A hyper-focus on achievement often comes at the expense of neglecting to teach invaluable traits that transcend time. Our high ground is seeing students for who they are and who they might become.

PUTTING IT INTO PRACTICE

Identify three things—above and beyond the formal curriculum—you feel called to impart upon your students. Write down your "Big 3" in the notes section in the back of this book. (My Big 3 while coaching included teaching student athletes about commitment, integrity, and attitude.)

After you have your Big 3, think about how you will authentically embed them into your classroom or school. The key is making them actionable by integrating them into work you're already doing. I didn't need to do a complete overhaul of the entire boys' soccer program to integrate my focus on commitment, integrity, and attitude; for example, most high school teams already order T-shirts. We just made sure our T-shirts celebrated the three character traits which we were committed to. The same went for our year-end awards banquet.

We figured that for every achievement-oriented awards category (e.g., MVP), we should add at least one category celebrating a soft skill or character trait. I've heard it said that what you give time to is what you love, so we dedicated equal time to celebrating players' achievements on and off the field. This same approach applies to our work in schools. I listed three of my current priorities as a principal on the next page. (See Figure 1.1.)

[Figure 1.1: Big Three Priorities]

BIG 3	ACTION IDEAS
EVERY PERSON A **PASSIONATE READER**	CREATE MONTHLY BOOKTALK VIDEOS TO SHARE MY PASSION FOR READING EMPOWER STUDENTS TO CREATE A PODCAST OR YOUTUBE CHANNEL SHARING BOOKS THEY'RE READING
EVERY LEARNER AN **INNOVATOR**	RESERVE A LINE ITEM IN OUR SCHOOL'S BUDGET TO SUPPORT INNOVATION; CONNECT DOLLARS TO STUDENT IDEAS
EACH LEARNER'S **TALENTS UNLEASHED**	PAIR A MENTOR WITH STUDENTS TO NURTURE THEIR PASSIONS AND UNEARTH HIDDEN TALENTS. (START SMALL WITH ONE OR TWO STUDENTS, AND GROW THE EFFORT OVER TIME) BE MORE INTENTIONAL ABOUT TAPPING INTO STUDENTS' TALENTS IN EVERY ASPECT OF SCHOOL, INCLUDING ASSEMBLIES, OFFICE COMMUNICATIONS, AND P.D.

HOW MIGHT YOU EMBED YOUR **BIG 3** INTO WORK YOU'RE ALREADY DOING?

Creating Conversation and Community

I'll never forget the conversations we had on our varsity coaching staff about how we wanted to cultivate character in our student athletes. The dialogue and commitments we made together truly changed the trajectories of some of our student athletes' lives. I'd like to invite you to reflect on the questions below and dialogue with others using the #ReclaimingOurCalling community hashtag. I can't wait to hear what you think.

1. How might we implement our Big 3 when it seems like we barely have time to teach the curriculum?
2. Joey's teachers made it clear there was a place for him in our school—and anyone paying attention could see their core beliefs in action. What steps have you taken to ensure your current work communicates why you said, "yes" to the students you serve?
3. How do you know when you're teaching from higher ground and pursuing learning that lasts?

#RECLAIMINGOURCALLING

CHAPTER 2

Ode to Kenny

Backstory

I'm not a car aficionado by any stretch, but there's something to be said for lifting the hood and checking out the size and condition of a car's engine. After all, it doesn't matter how shiny a vehicle is if the engine is in disrepair. The same holds true of education. We need to look beyond the surface to get a better understanding of what drives the deeper work we're destined to do. And we can't be afraid to share this work.

IF YOU COULD DO A "SHOW AND TELL" ABOUT SOMETHING IN YOUR CLASSROOM OR SCHOOL, WHAT WOULD YOU CHOOSE TO SHARE?

Kenny Mauer

Don't let the title of this chapter fool you. Kenny Mauer was a ticking time bomb to Joey. Whenever the two were in the same room—or on the same school bus—it was only a matter of time before Kenny unleashed all sorts of evil. I'm not exaggerating.

One school year, Kenny made a habit of sitting behind Joey and me on the bus ride home. (I still get sick to my stomach and a little teary-eyed thinking about this.) Every afternoon, Kenny would reach over the back of our seat and flick Joey in the ear as if he was flicking a crumb off the kitchen table. By the time our bus stop came, Joey's ear would be a humiliating shade of red. And I'd feel like the worst friend in the world.

I have so many fond memories from my childhood, but this is probably one of my biggest regrets. It never occurred to us to tell anyone what Kenny was doing. At the time, we thought our best option was hoping Kenny would be absent from school. It was horrible; however, it taught Joey and me a lesson about loyalty. After what we went through that year, we knew we'd never bail on one another. I even noticed Joey starting to look out for other kids when Kenny wasn't around.

It's important to note that the school-bus bullying we endured didn't define our entire childhood. I refuse to give Kenny that much power. And as an act of goodwill (albeit lukewarm), I'll

Try This!

On behalf of somebody who saw his best friend belittled (physically and mentally) on a regular basis, I offer this as a heartfelt plea: Find a way to check in with students on a regular basis. Make sure your check-ins go beyond surface-level pleasantries. I can't help but think Joey and I would have eventually built up the courage to confide in an adult had somebody checked in with us on a deeper level.

share something else Kenny did that actually taught me a lesson worth remembering.

Show and Tell was always a big deal to my friends and me. It was our time to shine. Our teachers would carve out a portion of the day when we were allowed to bring our favorite things to school. (I suppose you could say this was passion-based learning before that became a thing.)

I don't know if there were any rules about what we could or couldn't bring to Show and Tell although I'm sure some things were prohibited. My life revolved around all things LEGO, and I would occasionally bring photographs to share instead of the actual LEGO set I was working on.

I remember one particular Show and Tell like it was yesterday. I proudly strode across our classroom's cold, white tiles and handed my teacher a picture of my latest creation. My friends were seated in the corner of the room on carpet squares, eagerly awaiting the unveiling of my masterpiece.

I can still see their faces, but that's not all I remember.

When everyone saw my picture, they were filled with the standard Show-and-Tell questions. "How long did it take to build?" and "How many other LEGO sets do you have at home?" Then one of them asked, "Why don't you have a shirt on?"

Of course, I responded to their questions in order, and with the depth of knowledge only an eight-year-old can pull off:

"A long time."

"Lots."

"I don't know."

Truth be told, I hadn't considered why my shirt was missing until that moment. And thankfully, nobody seemed to pay much attention to the sticky note my mom had placed on the bottom of the picture.

Except Kenny Mauer.

As the rest of my classmates transitioned from Show and Tell to snack time, Kenny lingered near the bulletin board where my teacher had tacked up my special picture. And that's when my Show and Tell took on a life of its own.

Kenny's freckled face peeked underneath the sticky note and discovered what my mom was trying to conceal. It turns out the shirtless photo of me playing with a LEGO pirate ship captured how most of my Saturdays around the house looked when I was eight years old, underwear and all.

Exactly why my mom thought she should ever send a picture of me playing in my underwear to *school* is beyond me. Surely we had another picture of that forsaken pirate ship somewhere at home. (And instead of a sticky note, how about scissors?!)

To my mom's credit, it was a simpler time back then. Either way, the genie was out of the bottle, and Kenny Mauer had just reconvened a Show and Tell of his own with the rest of our class. He may have been obnoxious, but I actually give him credit for digging deeper.

Kenny's motives were almost always nefarious, but his curiosity showed he wasn't satisfied with surface-level sharing. He wanted the complete picture, especially since it contained a pair of Fruit of the Looms.

The lesson here is simple: School is not a complete picture of learning. Learning and our students' lives continue beyond the spaces we occupy together during the school day. When we look past some of the surface-level trappings of school and start to consider deeper drivers of learning, we get a more complete picture of our purpose.

Those of us who are blessed to work in schools each day know what's at the core of this profession. We don't need anyone to lift the veil, because we already understand what's beneath the surface. We live there. The problem is, there are people who have not stepped foot in a classroom since they were in school. And some of these people are making decisions about the future of education. Others are reporting on the state of education, and their narratives are often different from the reality we see in our classrooms and schools. You can see why this is problematic.

We need to help others develop a deeper understanding of the work we actually do. We need them to understand what's at the core and what we're capable of. To do this, we need to get better at helping them see what might not be outwardly evident. Basically, we need to channel our inner Kenny Mauer and help everyone see the whole picture.

Our Calling

On the surface, it may appear as if education is the vehicle for transferring vast amounts of information from one generation to the next. This was the function of education for centuries—and remained so even as many of us were students. Unfortunately, many people expect that same purpose to remain in place today. In reality, students are counting on us to teach them so much more than content.

We have a responsibility to help people see school as more than an artificial structure where kids consume surface-level content. We need to help them see the foundational layers of learning that aren't always apparent to the casual observer. The diagram on the next page provides a preview of what the moral foundation of our work looks like. (See Figure 2.1.) Call this my Ode to Kenny.

As I sat in my kitchen recently, reflecting on other professions that might have important (and unseen) layers, my daughter was working on some homework. She had been tasked with labeling the layers of the earth's crust and writing definitions for things like the *asthenosphere*. I challenged her by asking, "How do scientists really *know* the distinct layers of the earth exist since they've never actually seen the core?" This got us both thinking and diving into a Google search.

The Core of Our Calling

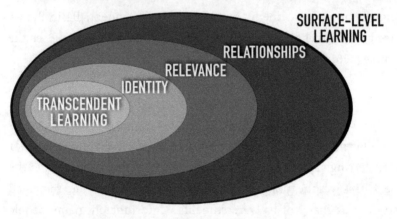

[Figure 2.1: The Core of Our Calling]

Did You Know?

Scientists study the different layers of the earth by observing sound waves emitted from earthquakes. There's a Global Seismographic Network with more than 150 seismic stations strategically positioned all over the world. These stations use state-of-the-art sensors to measure the intensity of sound waves.[1]

We also learned scientists are able to study more than just the intensity of sound waves. Anytime there's an earthquake, it's accompanied by a rapid release of energy. This energy travels a great distance, so scientists use multiple seismic stations to measure the sound waves. Most of this made sense to my daughter and me, but we were still left with wondering how scientists know so much about the different layers.

It turns out that the speed at which sound waves travel from station to station helps scientists determine the depths of the different layers of the earth's core. Any time a sound wave enters a new layer of the earth's crust, the sound wave bends due to the density change in that new layer.[2]

By no means am I an earthquake expert, but I do love learning new things. I discovered a fun classroom experiment that demonstrates how scientists can be so sure about the layers of the earth even though they cannot see them. (Stay with me; I promise there's a compelling point coming.)

1. Start by standing behind one end of a table. Next, lean over the table until your ear is touching the tabletop. (If you're anything like me, you will Clorox-wipe the table like crazy before attempting this experiment in your classroom.)

2. Next, have a trustworthy student stand at the opposite end of the table and carefully tap the table top. As your trustworthy student taps the table, you'll hear sound waves on your end of the table.

3. Now comes the fun part: Grab the biggest textbook or dictionary you can find and ask another student to press the book against the underside of the table. (The book represents another layer of the earth's crust.) Then ask your original trustworthy student to try tapping their end of the table again. This time you will hear a distinct difference in the sound because of the big book pressed underneath the table.

This experiment demonstrates how scientists study different layers that make up the core of the earth simply by measuring sound

Try This!

Try replicating the experiment above with your students or colleagues, only this time use the hands-on experiment as a powerful reminder about the importance of getting to know the hidden hopes, dreams, and fears others have. After conducting the experiment as a group, set aside time for smaller groups to share something most people might not notice if they don't look past the surface.

Voices from the Field

"One of my priorities is looking beyond traditional means of assessment and grading. Kids have learned how to play the game of school. Utilizing feedback and reflection pushes students to think more deeply, but most students stop learning after they receive a letter grade."

—Valerie Neuharth,
middle school social studies
teacher, South Dakota

waves.[3] They don't need to *see* the mantle, outer core, or inner core of the earth to know these layers exist.

Educators don't need to be able to *see* the most important things in education to know they exist. There's no disputing the unseen talents and other things stirring deep in the hearts and minds of students. These are the talents (when properly developed) that will help students be successful into their future. Surface-level learning alone is inadequate in preparing students for an unknown future.

Surface-Level Learning

If you've ever heard the phrase "a mile wide and an inch deep," you probably know where this is going. (See Figure 2.2.) When we try to cover too wide a breadth of content, we limit the time available for students to take their learning and curiosity deeper. It's a basic cause-and-effect relationship.

Covering a massive breadth of information diminishes our ability to teach the whole learner on a deeper level. Time and resources are in short supply, so we must use what we have wisely. People have been talking about depth and breadth in education for quite some time, so this is not entirely new. If anything, it's an affirmation to any educator pursuing learning that lasts.

We'll delve further into *how* to take things deeper next chapter. For now, I want us to take an honest look at the impact of spending so much time focusing on surface-level skills.

Depth vs. Breadth

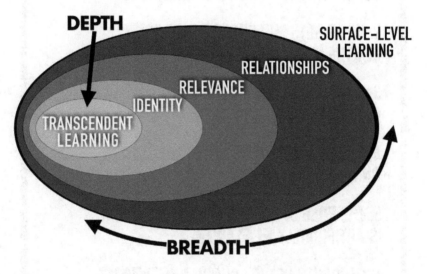

[Figure 2.2: Depth vs. Breadth]

When I was chatting with my daughter at our kitchen counter, I never questioned the importance of her learning information about science and social studies. I recognize there's value in knowing what an "asthenosphere" is and how many kilometers below the surface of the earth it is. At the same time, there's a vicious surface-learning cycle playing out in schools everywhere. When we only prioritize the things that are easiest to measure, we make it very difficult to pursue deeper learning experiences. Here's how the surface-level learning cycle plays out:

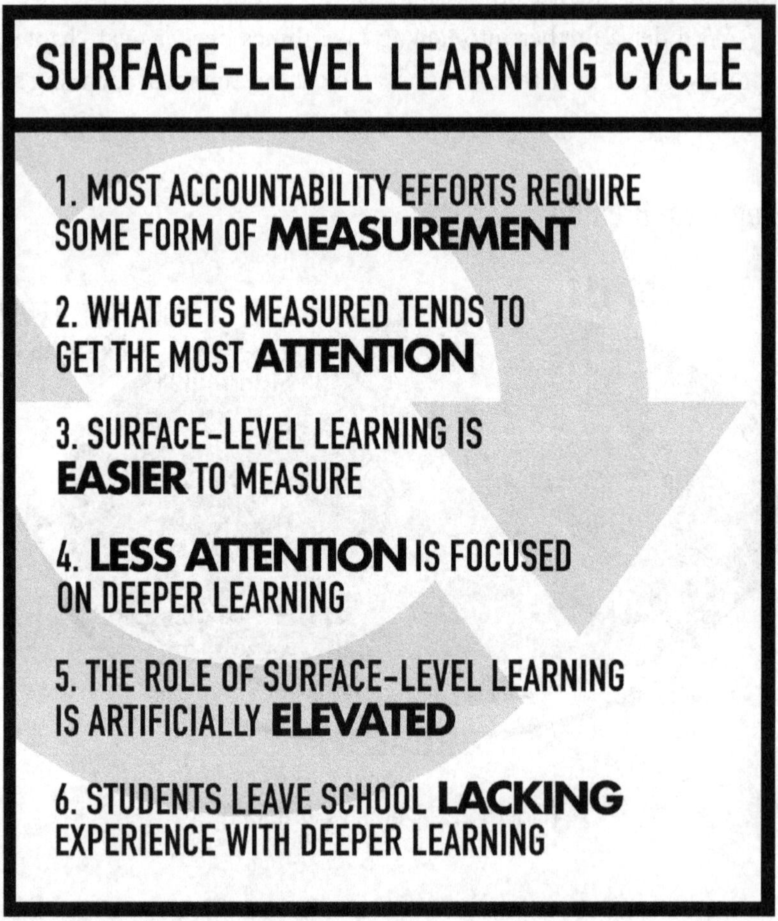

SURFACE-LEVEL LEARNING CYCLE

1. MOST ACCOUNTABILITY EFFORTS REQUIRE SOME FORM OF **MEASUREMENT**

2. WHAT GETS MEASURED TENDS TO GET THE MOST **ATTENTION**

3. SURFACE-LEVEL LEARNING IS **EASIER** TO MEASURE

4. **LESS ATTENTION** IS FOCUSED ON DEEPER LEARNING

5. THE ROLE OF SURFACE-LEVEL LEARNING IS ARTIFICIALLY **ELEVATED**

6. STUDENTS LEAVE SCHOOL **LACKING** EXPERIENCE WITH DEEPER LEARNING

[Figure 2.3: Surface-Level Learning Cycle]

This cycle creates a void in the exact place where students are longing for deeper, transferable learning experiences—that place is school. If the cycle persists, education will become less and less meaningful to the students we serve.

Analogous to Teaching

My dad passed away several years ago, but I remember one evening he and I had been tasked with grabbing take-out food for the rest of the family. As we strode through the dimly lit front doors of dad's favorite Chinese restaurant, he noticed some fresh-cut flowers sitting on the tables.

Being the hopeless romantic he was, he tried bartering for some of the flowers when paying for our pot stickers and sweet-and-sour chicken. There must have been a bit

Voices from the Field

"Too often, schooling is a series of tasks students must complete in order to move to the next grade level. If tasks seem to have little or no connection to the real world, students become disengaged. In order to reach deeper learning, assignments should ask students to become contributors rather than consumers. The goal is to see how students can demonstrate understanding in multiple ways."

—**Steven Weber**,
associate superintendent,
Arkansas

of a language barrier because, even at a young age, I could tell dad's negotiation for the flowers was failing fast. A restaurant employee kept responding to his requests with the same perplexing question: "You'll bring them back?"

Neither of us understood why we would give my stepmom flowers and then bring the flowers back to the restaurant. It made no sense, but my dad was not easily dissuaded. After negotiating for several minutes, the employee relented, "Just take the flowers, but be sure to bring them back."

Our confusion shifted to anticipation as we carried our food and a vase of bright purple flowers out to the car. I fastened my seatbelt and started rifling through the take-out bags to make sure we had everything. That's when I noticed we got more than we bargained for.

The flowers came with a generous coating of dust. The employee had been reluctant to let us take the flowers home because they were fake (and probably part of the permanent restaurant decor). My dad and I laughed so hard at our failure to notice the obvious!

Sometimes I wonder if we might be unknowingly living out a similar fake-flower negotiation in education. The very things that appear real to us in one setting, like those flowers, lose their luster when seen in a different light. In other words, our students may not see the same connection and value in the content and pedagogy we adults are prioritizing. I know I'm as guilty as the next person of modeling practices that feel authentic to me but seem less real to others. Sometimes I mistakenly assume a base level of buy-in, relevance, or understanding is present where confusion or apathy really exist.

Here's an example most educators can relate to: Have you ever asked a group, "Does that make sense?" or "Does anyone have any questions?" We know these questions are not the best to elicit feedback, but they've become ingrained in our vernacular. These questions and the responses they elicit may feel meaningful to us, but through the lens of the learner they are like the dusty, old flowers my dad and I drove home with. They don't really pass the fake-flower test.

Sometimes I'll try asking, "What questions do you have?" to be more inviting to anyone who might actually have a question. When combined with ample wait time, this subtle change in wording tends to elicit a little more feedback. Asking more authentic questions will provide an opportunity to take learning to a new level, but there are strategies to further engage learners.

Don't be dismayed if your questioning practices (or any other element of your work) has left some people feeling as if they were holding fake flowers. The context in which kids are growing up is ever changing. Reflecting on relevance and increasing the authenticity of our practices is an ongoing process. It points out the legitimacy of the term "lifelong learner."

Whether you agree with the basic premise or feel frustrated at the lack of time and support to do anything about it, our students need us to break the surface-learning cycle; otherwise, we run the risk of missing an opportunity to grow along with our students.

Try This!

Try taking your checks for understanding deeper. The next time you want to see how well a group understands something, invite them to explain the first few steps to a partner. You might also ask learners to evaluate what they anticipate being the most challenging part of a project or invite them to generate divergent approaches with a partner. Listening to these conversations may provide some of the most authentic feedback you hear.

Joey Forrest

I mentioned my friend Joey being one of the fastest students in our grade level growing up, but I don't think I conveyed just how competitive he was. I think that's why we got along so well. No matter who we were hanging out with, Joey would somehow find a way to escalate conversations until they became random athletic competitions.

When we were younger, the contests usually involved friendly foot races during recess. As we grew up, we were just as likely to challenge each other to races in the shopping mall parking lot. It's true. One minute we'd be killing time in the food court, and the next we'd be lined up in a sprinter's stance in the parking lot of the mall.

Seriously, who does that? (The answer is *anyone Joey Forrest is hanging out with*.)

Given Joey's impressive speed, I suppose it was only a matter of time before he bailed on me and the rest of our high school tennis team. He made the switch over to track and field his sophomore year. And I thank my lucky stars I was there to see his first preseason track meet.

Joey was running the 400-meter dash, which he was quick to point out was the longest sprint there is in track and field. I remember two things about Joey's first real race: the color of the track (bright blue) and the spectacle that occurred at the finish line.

As Joey approached the finish line, he leaned forward toward the tape, just like we always pretended to do when we raced outside during recess. Only this wasn't the same as our short recess jaunts. As Joey leaned forward it became painfully obvious he had absolutely no strength left in his legs. His lean turned into a face-first tumble.

Joey's face-plant was one for the ages. His nose hit the ground just before reaching the finish line, so technically, I'm not even sure he finished his first race. As you can imagine, his new high school track teammates had a field day with jokes about the "rookie" crashing and burning. I have to admit it was hilarious. I laughed along with them, but only because I knew Joey would bounce back. He always did.

In a strange way, educators tend to make the same mistake Joey did. Sometimes we lean toward a finish line called "surface-level learning." It's our own real-life fake flower.

And just like Joey, there's a fundamental flaw in our technique. We should be operating with our feet

Try This!

Grab a sticky note and write down one thing you want to stand firm on every time you get to work, teach a lesson, or start a staff meeting. Keep that note where you'll see it each day. You'll be amazed at how you can transform your thinking and build better habits simply by reminding yourself of where you want to stand.

firmly planted on the moral foundation of teaching instead of leaning toward the things that are easiest to measure. The moral foundation of teaching is our high ground, and we need to stand firm on it.

I know principals who write personal reminders to themselves like, "5–2" near their office workstations. In this specific example, the numbers represent the goal of having at least five meaningful conversations with individual staff members and writing two personal thank-you notes each day. When we remind ourselves of what is real and write down what we want to stand firm on, we're more likely to follow through.

Mrs. MacLean

Mrs. MacLean kept a note on her lesson-planning book that read, "Students first." Even though we worked closely together for several months while I was teaching, I never asked her about that sticky note. I didn't need to. Her focus was obvious in everything she did. Even in contentious meetings, she lived those words without holding them over everyone else's head.

Through the years, I've reflected on what made Mrs. MacLean so effective and magnetic. She did so many things well, but a few of her practices still stand out in my memory after all these years, like the way she built relationships with kids, got them excited about reading, and readily shared her passion for puzzles.

Like magic, Mrs. MacLean's strengths and passions seamlessly supported her students. She deftly used reading and riddles as a means to build relationships, but the converse was also true: She used relationships to help students fall in love with reading (and riddles). I can't explain it other than to say her ability to build relationships with students and staff was different from anything I had observed up until that point. And by "different," I mean deeper.

Mrs. MacLean taught me that students appreciate when we let our guard down and share our idiosyncrasies with them. She loved a good brain teaser. It didn't matter if it was a riddle, puzzle, or intriguing story, she shared them regularly with her students and somehow related them to her lessons. She even embedded Easter eggs and secret messages at the very end of books and assignments.

I wasn't particularly adept at analyzing pedagogy or articulating why something was effective back then, but it didn't take a rocket scientist to see how her approach had students begging for more. I'm actually borrowing one of her brain teasers because it foreshadows where we're going in the chapters that follow. (See Figure 2.4.) Keep in mind, Mrs. MacLean had a younger clientele, so you might be disappointed if you're looking for a super-complex challenge; however, this might give you a glimpse of why students loved her so much.

When she introduced this puzzle to our class, I found myself just as engaged as students. Being the ridiculously good teacher she was, Mrs. MacLean gave everyone paper drinking cups to physically slide around while we discussed how to create an alternating pattern of full/empty glasses.

After the lesson, she explained to me how progressing from concrete to abstract helped students internalize important concepts. Only Mrs. MacLean could weave in Piaget without it feeling forced or condescending. She was a machine.

The best teachers are purposeful about almost everything. If you stop to ask them why they do what they do (even down to the most seemingly insignificant decision), they will usually be able to explain how it was either helping an individual student or proactively setting another student up for success.

Back to the brain teasers.

THE THREE GLASSES ON THE LEFT ARE FULL, AND THE THREE ON THE RIGHT ARE EMPTY.

MOVING ONLY **ONE** GLASS, MAKE A ROW OF ALTERNATELY FULL AND EMPTY GLASSES.

Image: Adapted from a popular logic puzzle

[Figure 2.4: Empty Glasses Brainteaser[4]]

Mrs. MacLean believed brain teasers had the ability to push thinking to a different plane, one on which we're not accustomed to operating. In doing so, she helped create new mental models that compelled students to see solutions where they once only saw barriers.

In case you were wondering, I've included a solution to her paper cup brain teaser at the end of this chapter. (See Figure 2.5.) You should also know you and I are a lot like those glasses. (The full ones, not the empty ones.) Educators already have what it takes to facilitate learning that lasts. The solution is inside us; we just need to share it.

PUTTING IT INTO PRACTICE

Lest we forget how Kenny Mauer corrupted my Show and Tell moment, I want to circle back to the concept of sharing once more, only this time I'll focus on the power of connecting over things that matter. In all my years as an educator, I don't recall a single time when a student brought something in for Show and Tell that wasn't meaningful to them. Students use the opportunity and platform given to them to share what's important to them.

Think about a moment that touched your heart as an educator. (It doesn't need to be a big story or grandiose set of circumstances.) Whatever moment you choose, don't shy away from why it's of deeper importance to you. Your moment might be about a time you made a difference for a student or helped a colleague grow.

Once you've reflected for a bit, write down that memory. Peel back the layers and share some of the thinking and context that might not be outwardly evident to another educator who reads your small-moment story. In some ways, this is an opportunity for you to participate in a professional version of Show and Tell.

> *We should stop shying away from the work we do that's having a deeper impact; we wouldn't want our students to shy away from their success and struggles, and we shouldn't either.*

Creating Conversation and Community

Educators have a responsibility to practice and model sharing. When we show others how we're learning and connecting with students on a deeper level, we open ourselves up to building community where it did not previously exist. You never know when your story might inspire somebody else who might be feeling as if they're working in a silo.

When we share, silos turn into cities.

I invite you to stretch yourself by sharing your story using a different tool or approach than how you typically communicate. This could involve creating a display, starting a blog, or participating in an informal exchange prior to a staff meeting. The important thing is that you share your small-moment story and invite others to join the conversation as well.

1. What is the best thing that could happen if each of us started sharing more of our small-moment stories and reflecting on the stories other educators are sharing?

2. To what degree do the parents in your school know how you are taking learning deeper? How will you and your district share your efforts to stand on the moral foundation of teaching?

3. In what ways could we model purposeful sharing so students like Kenny have an opportunity to see how it's done with integrity and relevance?

#ReclaimingOurCalling

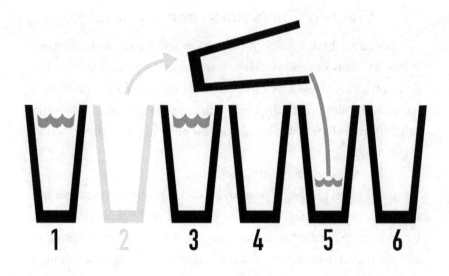

Image: Adapted from a popular logic puzzle

[Figure 2.5: Empty Glasses Solution]

Resources

1. "GSN – Global Seismographic Network," *USGS*, earthquake.usgs.gov/monitoring/gsn.

2–3. "How Do Scientists Know about the Different Earth Layers If They Can't Go There?" *USCB ScienceLine*, 04/01/2001, scienceline.ucsb.edu/getkey.php?key=3249.

4. "Brain Teaser: Care to Play a Game of Tumblers?" *Passnownow.com*, passnownow.com/brain-teaser-care-to-play-a-game-of-tumblers.

CHAPTER 3

Acts of Intentionality

Backstory

The *moral foundation of education* is built upon relationships and learning that lasts. Pushing past surface learning and into deeper, transcendent learning experiences is possible. How we're teaching and reaching the whole learner through relationships, relevance, identity, and transcendent learning is the core of our calling.

WHAT ARE THE THINGS YOU DO AS AN EDUCATOR THAT INITIATE ENTRY-LEVEL RELATIONSHIPS WITH STUDENTS, AND HOW DO YOU MOVE TOWARD ESTABLISHING DEEPER CONNECTIONS?

Liz

That fateful observation Liz conducted in our classroom occurred during the spring of one of my first years of teaching. I may have made Liz's observation sound like a classic case of helicopter parenting, but I really don't want us to look at her visit that way.

She was trying to make an important decision on behalf of her son. Somewhat surprisingly, she must have seen something positive during her visit to our classroom, because that observation wasn't the last time I saw Liz. Her son was placed on my class roster the following year, and she became one of the most amazing parent volunteers I have ever known. I've since learned that her decision to place her son in my classroom was a relational one. She observed me tapping into relationships to take student learning deeper, something I learned from watching Mrs. MacLean use head-to-heart connections nearly every lesson.

Liz turned out to be a godsend to me and my class early in my career when I was less efficient, and every single thing I encountered came with a steep learning curve. Liz was an extra set of hands, eyes, and caring presence in our classroom. The time she gave so freely allowed me to be more present to my students. I don't think it's any coincidence she showed up week after week and was able to help us out in such a meaningful manner; in fact, she was very intentional about her support.

Start with Relationships

Liz understood the key to classroom relationships before I was ever able to articulate it as an educator. The most gifted educators connect in a manner that's *meaningful to the other person*. This sounds easy enough, but sometimes it feels like there's an invisible push to skim past building authentic connections with kids. The invisible push could be a shortage of time or pressure to cover content. This pressure, or the perception thereof, makes it even more important to be intentional about staying grounded in the relationships that drive all learning.

When the frenetic pace of school kicks in, it can be difficult to develop the relationships required to facilitate learning that lasts. With time in short supply, the wide breadth of content we're required to cover can have us spinning in circles rather than in the direction we really want to go.

My family had a membership to a nearby campground as I was growing up. Every weekend we'd pile into the car and tow a small pop-up camper cramped with coolers, sleeping bags, and firewood. Evenings at the campground consisted of roasting marshmallows, storytelling, and the occasional game of charades. I'll never forget the time my dad tried acting out the song "Moon River" during a charades game. (I'm just thankful he started with the second word and we successfully guessed the song before the inevitable.)

Try This!

Start a class or staff meeting by connecting with people regarding something that's important to them. Invite others to find a photo on their cell phone that shows a special time, place, or person. Next, have them share with somebody in the room who they don't connect with on a regular basis. This simple act creates community and takes relationships deeper. (Thanks to Jimmy Casas for sharing this idea!)

Dad's shenanigans weren't reserved for the evening hours. He competed in the annual campground horseshoe tournament—wearing only a Speedo and cowboy boots. (A wardrobe decision I vowed *never* to repeat.) As colorful as some of those moments were, most of our time around the lake involved fishing and anything else a kid could dream of doing on the water.

My parents even had a friend at the campground who invented a new recreational watercraft. She found a small-scale manufacturer, and our campground ordered several units to rent to fellow campers. It seemed everyone was buzzing about the bright-yellow floating contraptions.

A single rider would stand atop the watercraft and rock back and forth. The swaying motion caused two giant flippers underneath the watercraft to propel a passenger forward. I asked one of my kids to draw a diagram of the contraption so you have a better idea of what I'm talking about. (See Figure 3.1.)

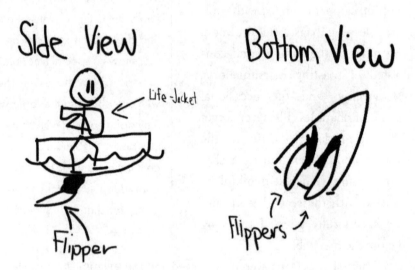

[Figure 3.1: Campground Invention Illustration]

One day my sister and I rented a couple units and dragged them into the water. My sister stood up and immediately started gliding toward deeper water. I began to rock back and forth as well, only instead of going forward, my watercraft started spinning in circles.

Doing circles in the shallow water while my sister was joyriding across the lake frustrated me to no end. I recently asked my mom about this, and like any good parent, she was able to produce a photograph circa 1985. (See Figure 3.2.)

[Figure 3.2: Campground Invention Photograph]

If you look closely at the picture you can even see my sister in the background as she's gliding away from the camera while I hold my arms up in exasperation. Not long after Mom snapped this picture, I waded back to shore and pleaded my case to a campground employee.

Try This!

Make a point to acknowledge your students' passions and interests when calling on them during discussions; for example, if you're having a conversation about grammar, you might mention a particular student's interest in writing before hearing what they have to contribute. If you have a history buff in class, you might acknowledge their past contributions before seeking a historical perspective on the topic at hand. By intentionally integrating the unique interests of students into conversations, we champion learning that lasts.

The employee flipped the contraption upside down and discovered the problem. Somebody had installed one of the flippers backwards, and that was causing my watercraft to spin in circles.

A similar phenomenon is happening right now in schools everywhere.

The influence of high-stakes testing coupled with the vast amount of surface-level content we're required to cover creates a gravitational pull toward surface-level learning. Deeper learning has not been the only casualty either. Our relationships have become improperly aligned with surface-level work due to this pull. It doesn't have to be this way.

Mrs. MacLean's Secret

Mrs. MacLean established relationships based on the unique interests and passions of the learners she served. In this way, she was able to resist the persistent pull toward surface-level learning. She shared her passions with others, and we looked for ways to celebrate hers in return. This was evidenced by the different puzzles and books she received as gifts during the holidays.

As cool as all the problem-solving and riddles were, it was her commitment to people that seemed to underpin everything she did.

I'll be honest and say I feel a little like that kindergarten student who says, "You're the best teacher ever" when I say this, but as a teacher, I couldn't have asked for a better mentor. When given the choice, she always chose relationships and depth.

Like Mrs. MacLean, each of us has a choice to make. (See Figure 3.3.) Imagine what schools could be for students if we started with relationships and committed to working toward learning that lasts. That would be one heck of a course correction!

IT **STARTS** WITH RELATIONSHIPS

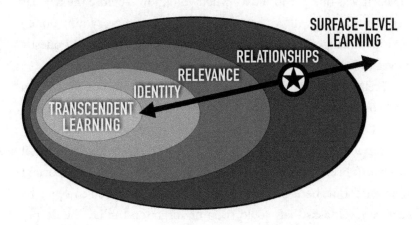

[Figure 3.3: Reimagining Relationships]

We must break the cycle of taking right turns toward surface-level learning. When we start with relationships and practice acts of intentionality, we honor the whole learner and make transcendent learning possible. With regular practice, we develop a rhythm and cadence in our work making relational learning as intuitive as Mrs. MacLean made it look.

Reimagining Relationships

Even though the team I serve on is developing this flow now, it can still feel like chasing unicorns on crazier days, not to mention during testing season. Time seems to be one of the rarest commodities in a school. As a principal, I find there are more requests for meetings than minutes in a day.

And email. Ugh.

Being intentional about my mindset, specifically when it comes to investing in relationships, has made a huge difference for me. But this wasn't always the case.

I remember rushing down a hallway in my first year as a principal. (It was one of those days when you know—before the day has begun—that you will not have enough time to get everything done.) A student caught my attention because she needed help. I honestly forget what she needed, but I remember stopping to help her.

Feeling frustrated that I wasn't getting anything done, I put a smile on my face as I chatted with her until she looked up at me and said, "I'm so glad you were here." She was beaming.

Boom. In that moment I realized I *was* getting something done; it just hadn't been written down on my to-do list. This was an important moment for me because I realized my to-do list had been co-opted by surface-level tasks that would soon be forgotten (unlike the deeper connection I had just made with the student).

"The conversation is the work."

I recently read that quote, although I don't know whom to attribute it to. The quote resonated so much that I made a copy and placed it near my workstation. The important work of building relationships is done through conversation. It's accomplished by being present and creating a space for students to be curious. These are the conditions that allow us to take relationships deeper instead of being pulled toward surface-level learning. I'm still striving to grow in this area, but I know intentionality is helping.

Taking relationships deeper isn't a checklist-type endeavor. You might try one of the examples to the right and realize it doesn't work for you. That's great! Lesson learned. Whatever you decide to do, do it with intentionality.

Relevance Isn't Optional

Being intentional about relationships alone doesn't guarantee deeper learning will occur. Relevance is also required.

Many districts already have processes intended to keep curriculum current, but just because a well-defined curriculum is in place doesn't mean students will experience it in a relevant manner. This reminds me of something I've heard George Couros share. (See Figure 3.4.)

Try This!

Here are a few ways I've seen teachers practice acts of intentionality while resisting the pull of surface-level stuff.

1. Connect with individual students and their families using handwritten notes, short phone calls, an occasional lunch in the classroom, or attendance at extracurricular activities.

2. Include students in authentic tasks you're responsible for completing. Try creating classroom or school video newsletters with groups of students instead of writing newsletters alone.

3. Cultivate connections over time by sending positive postcards before or after the school year. One teacher I know invites former students back for class reunions. They play games, eat snacks, and enjoy catching up.

#INNOVATORSMINDSET

THE CURRICULUM TELLS YOU "WHAT" NOT "HOW." THE **HOW** IS THE ARTISTRY IN EDUCATION.

GEORGE COUROS

[Figure 3.4: The Curriculum Tells You "What"]

The only thing I would add to George's sentiments is the importance of starting with *who*. The "what" and "how" come alive when we know *whom* we're serving. That's relevance.

I don't think it's a coincidence the same teachers who build deeper relationships with students are also able to make the learning process meaningful to individual learners. They are gifted *noticers* who prioritize listening, asking open-ended questions, and learning about students' interests outside of school. These teachers understand the importance of *who*. This helps them ensure their approach is always relevant.

When we train ourselves to look, listen, and question, we will notice just how connected students have become. They are growing up in a world where information gathering and social sharing occur simultaneously. Communication today is much more networked than what I experienced growing up.

If we're not providing students access to the tools, skills, and options they appreciate, they will seek out relevance on their own. Students value having a say in "how" they learn—just as most of the educators I know appreciate having a voice in their professional development. Relevance can no longer be assumed based solely upon our expert opinion. We can't rely solely on our own training and experience, because we were born in a different time. Our beliefs and biases about school and what constitutes learning will be significantly different from that of students who will never know a world without Bluetooth, streaming, and Wi-Fi. If you've ever observed a child learning a new skill by watching videos online, you know what I'm talking about.

We would do well to notice and tap into this phenomenon of networked social learning as well as our students' desire to participate—and contribute to—this connected ecosystem. Staying relevant, however, might require us to get unstuck from some of the methods and routines we've become attached to.

Voices from the Field

"How can teachers deepen student thinking beyond initial responses? Could creating and celebrating a culture of questions work? How might discussions improve if we emphasized 'What else could this mean?' over 'I think that...'? A classroom where students are explicitly taught to ask good questions will always lead to deeper, more critical thinking."

—**Anne-Marie Hanson**, high school English teacher, Manitoba, Canada

Analogous to Teaching

My wife and a few close friends arranged a special trip to Nashville to celebrate my fortieth birthday. We spent the weekend touring Music City and catching up with one another. One of my favorite moments was shopping for cowboy boots together.

I learned a couple things about myself during our boot-shopping excursion, and one of them relates to relevance. First, I learned I look pretty good in python-skin cowboy boots. Second, it is exceedingly difficult to remove a cowboy boot from your foot.

Seriously difficult.

A cowboy boot glides *on* with ease, but you basically need to dislocate an ankle to get the boot off—unless you're comfortable asking an innocent bystander to help pry the boot off. (This option can lead to awkward moments at airport security checkpoints when traveling alone.)

When we think about how we teach and reach our learners, we need to ensure we don't wear our routines like a pair of cowboy boots. In other words, we need to be sure it's not an ankle-busting effort to update our approach. We need to be nimble enough to make changes so our "how" is always relevant to the people we are serving.

The tools and approach we use should always reflect the passions and needs of the students we serve. Your students are uniquely created and different from the students I serve, so I'm not about to get overly prescriptive; besides, the moment we start to identify specific tools,

Try This!

Try taking off your "cowboy boots," or ask somebody to help you take them off! Connect with a co-worker or somebody in your network to talk about pedagogy and the "who" and "how" of teaching. Be intentional about using the conversation as a catalyst to update part of your practice.

they're probably on their way to becoming obsolete. Interestingly enough, the changing nature of technology is one of the excuses some educators use for *not* updating their methods, myself included.

When Virtual Reality (VR) first came onto the scene, I didn't really understand the hype, so I dismissed the technology altogether. For me, VR seemed like a flashy version of the "next best thing." I wasn't hearing anyone talk about VR in terms of pedagogy or how it supported deeper learning.

It wasn't until my son wanted to go to a VR arcade at the Mall of America for his birthday party that I understood what the draw might be. As my son and I made our way around the arcade, we played almost fifty immersive VR games. The experience was absolutely breathtaking, and all the graphics were stunningly beautiful. I was so impressed by the immersive nature of the games that I predicted VR would play a major role in recreation and learning within the next five years. Needless to say, technology has really evolved since 1985 and the days of my Atari 2600 video game system.

So what might the evolution of gaming mean for schools, in pedagogical terms?

We can't allow the disconnect between the technology and games students enjoy outside of school to grow. We all need to strive to help students create and connect in ways that are meaningful to them now and into their future. But ensuring learning experiences are relevant has to be more purposeful than placing new technology into students' hands. Students need to own the process and audience for their learning. And a pedagogy that prioritizes student ownership will always put students in a position to create more than they consume.

As an example of prioritizing student ownership through content creation, our school started to look at VR differently. We knew the pinnacle of student learning was not strapping a cardboard viewfinder on a child's head and streaming premade VR content to them.

We invested in a 360-degree camera to empower students to create and share their own VR videos in multiple classes and content areas.

Remember: This is a story about a relevant pedagogy and has very little to do with any specific technology. Tools will come and go, so don't let a device define you as an educator. When given the choice between tech-savvy and learning-savvy, always err on the side of learning. The technology will follow.

When I present at conferences, one of my favorite conversation starters centers on the Mona Lisa image on the next page. (See Figure 3.5.) I start by challenging people to find at least ten discrepancies between the two Mona Lisa images, and I only give them thirty seconds to do so. (This challenge is easier when the image is projected on a large screen, but we can make this work.)

Before you keep reading, check out the picture and then pause to see if you can spot 10 differences in 30 seconds or less.

CAN YOU SPOT **10** DIFFERENCES?

Solution: Tree on right, her smile, hand position, number of river turns, nose shadow, horizon slope, sewing on sleeve, missing ring, crooked shawl, iPad.

[Figure 3.5: Mona Lisa Comparison]

How did you do? Although it appears the solution is listed directly beneath the two portraits, the real answer is different than you might think. The only difference between the Mona Lisa on the left and the Mona Lisa on the right is the iPad one of them is holding. That's it.

I share this because the Mona Lisa who is holding the iPad is not superior to the Mona Lisa without the device. Can I get an amen?!

Try This!

Try asking for student feedback on the tools and approaches you're using. (Don't ask if you're not open to receiving feedback or making changes.) Consider whether students would choose the tools or approaches when they're outside of school. If not, your pedagogy might not be as relevant as you'd like it to be.

69

There is another point that's equally important: The Mona Lisa without the device is not automatically better either. So before you become enamored with a new technology, try falling in love with a learner-driven pedagogy. And before you resist a new technology for whatever legitimate reasons you might have, try falling in love with a learner-driven pedagogy. Deeper learning is possible when the tools and approaches we're using are relevant to students.

The Importance of Identity

The simple act of getting to know a student might be the most profound thing we do as educators for many reasons, not the least of which is creating relevant learning experiences. I'd go so far as to say if we invested the majority of our professional learning time into getting to know our students, we would eventually be leading the most relevant learning institutions in the world.

Students' abilities, beliefs, cultures, families, mental health, hopes, and dreams help shape who they are. Some of these things may change over time, and others remain relatively constant. That's why knowing the identity of the whole learner is much more important than merely understanding a student's academic level or demographic data.

Here's another way to look at this: Although we find ourselves in a system that often associates a student's name with a number or designation, every child is a compilation of stories. Our job is to unearth the stories while recognizing the many strengths and needs that accompany them.

Knowing the Learner

Tapping into the stories that shape a student's identity starts with learning students' names and understanding their hobbies, but it doesn't stop there. During a conversation with an educator who was feeling frustrated with a student's choices, I realized part of the problem was the teacher didn't know who the student was yet. The school year had just started, so there had not been a lot of time to create a connection. This meant she was unsure of the student's interests outside of school and wasn't really sure how to reach the child.

As I listened to the teacher share, I moved into a place of deeper empathy. After all, how many principals can say they know all the interests of every staff member? When the teacher finished sharing, I couldn't help but notice how hard she was being on herself for not knowing the struggling student better. That's when I shared a short story about a *unique* parent phone call I'd had. (And when I use the term "unique," I mean career jolting.)

Come to think of it, the phone call felt more like taking smelling salts than anything else. It was a real wake-up call for me mostly because it helped me understand a weakness of mine through the eyes of a parent who knew her child much better than I. I had not been nearly as intentional as I should have been in getting to know this parent's child—and the child was struggling as a result. I want to hit more upon the importance of identity right now, so I will circle back to the specifics of this parent phone call in Chapter Five.

Many people talk about the importance of relationships, but few share specifics on how to understand and celebrate a student's identity. Many of the strategies I use to learn about students' identities are gleaned from what teachers share with me during interviews. I remember one applicant sharing a story about a home visit that helped her understand more about a student's family, faith, and cultural identity. I was impressed at how easy she made the concept of home visits sound and found myself convinced I should be connecting with families in spaces that are important to *them*.

Around that same time, our school's equity team was having conversations about student identity. We became aware that some of our Muslim students felt they needed to check their identity at the door for fear of being misunderstood or judged. As a result of our team's conversations, we reached out to some families, and a deeper dialogue ensued.

We were even invited to their local community center and place of worship. The families were visibly moved that we cared enough about knowing their children that we would meet with them in a space so central to their lives. I'll admit I felt a little out of place in such a different environment from what I was accustomed to; for example, at one point during the tour a sign directed us to remove our shoes before entering a sacred space. I'd never been asked to take off my shoes at church before, but to these families, our willingness to honor their culture and traditions meant we honored who they were.

Moments after removing my shoes, I noticed one of my dress socks had a huge hole, and my big toe was conspicuously sticking out. Talk about embarrassing! Eventually we transitioned to another room, and I was able to put my shoes back on. All embarrassment aside, that visit and some of the follow-up work we did together helped our team learn more about our students' identities than we might have learned over the course of an entire school year. For starters, we came to the realization that our school had to become a space where all stories are valued.

> *We need to enter into our students' world, wherever they might be, and seek to understand who we can become to serve them better.*

All Means ALL

Learning about a student's identity is only the beginning; we also need to use research-based practices supporting how individual students learn best. Thanks to the research of Zaretta Hammond, I'm beginning to understand some of the cognitive scaffolding all students bring with them to school. This scaffolding is a tremendous asset that can easily be overlooked if we're unaware it exists. Basically we can leverage how an individual student's brain has been hardwired to make learning stickier.[1]

Storytelling is one of the most brain-friendly and culturally proficient tools we can use. Storytelling connects content to neural pathways that have been developed over time and across multiple generations. It leverages the brain's memory systems, making it possible for students to create connections to the things relevant to them. When we use story we also tap into the oral traditions of many students whose families come from cultures with rich oral traditions.[1-3]

Try This!

We can't assume to know a student's story without asking, and we shouldn't assume a student will be comfortable sharing either. Try to take time to be more vulnerable sharing who you are, and provide a safe space for students to do the same. (In the event a student is sharing something off-topic or at an inopportune time, be intentional about circling back and listening later.)

Letting Go and Thinking Differently

You might be wondering what storytelling in the classroom looks like (especially if you don't consider yourself a storyteller). So let me tell you a story:

During a meeting with a new teacher for an observation preconference, I learned the teacher was planning to introduce a mathematical concept to her primary-grade students by introducing a learning target and transitioning to an anticipatory set. During our conversation, I referenced Zaretta Hammond's research on culturally proficient teaching strategies, and we started talking about how we might be able to use storytelling to engage students during the introduction of her math lesson. Our attention shifted to other components of the observation, and eventually the preconference meeting concluded.

The following day, I showed up in her classroom for the observation. I will admit to being more than a little curious to see how she was going to start the lesson, and whether or not she'd try telling a story. It wasn't long before she launched into a story about her younger brother sledding as a child. I was completely engrossed as she shared some additional details and then made a seamless connection to the math concept her class would be learning.

As I looked around, I noticed her students were just as engaged as I was. After the lesson, I met with the teacher for a post conference. We both agreed that for that particular lesson, the learning became sticky for everyone in the room. By thinking differently about her lesson hook, we were able to tap into the power of storytelling as a tool to connect with all learners.

For what it's worth, I try to start staff meetings off with a personal story that somehow connects to the topic or work at hand. Over time, I've noticed how sharing more about who I am has led to some special connections and follow-up from our team.

Transcendent Learning

The last layer in the core of our calling is transcendent learning. When I use the term *transcendent learning*, I'm talking about learning that lasts. This learning encapsulates the skills, experiences, and knowledge that matters most to students today and into their future. Some of the skills and knowledge students need to learn changes rapidly, and other skills remain just as important as they were decades ago.

Transcendent learning involves social-emotional learning and the skills students need to regulate their bodies and communicate effectively. It also includes the dispositions and character-building experiences that uniquely position students for a lifetime of learning. To better understand transcendent learning, we can look to the parts of an apple.

When I was in high school, I worked at a local apple orchard for several seasons. Apples were quickly sorted by size and appearance; for example, if a peeling was shiny and blemish free, we would place the apple in a basket labeled "firsts." If a peeling showed signs of cloudiness or bruising, it would be considered a "second" or possibly even a "cider-grade" apple.

Our sorting techniques relied upon quick aesthetic evaluations, but we weren't able to factor in the parts of the apple that matter even

Voices from the Field

"With everything in education (i.e., standards, technology, pedagogy, etc.) constantly changing, I place a high priority on timeless skills I believe my students will need after they leave our classroom. We practice soft skills like holding the door for someone, shaking hands, giving eye contact, and asking follow-up questions. We also practice the positive and powerful responsibility of digital citizenship by actually running our student-led Twitter and Instagram accounts @topdogkids during our school day."

—**Kayla Delzer**, elementary school teacher and CEO of Top Dog Teaching, Inc., North Dakota more. An apple's flesh determines its essence and character, and its seeds are capable of transcending time. And so it is with education.

The work we do, cultivating character and nourishing the ideals passed from one generation to another, is truly transcendent. Unfortunately, many educators are hearing the message that caring about a child's core cannot coexist with high expectations for student achievement. This couldn't be further from the truth. Teaching the whole learner involves both academic achievement *and* ensuring students carry seeds of success with them long after they leave our schools.

Voices from the Field

"As a teacher, I get to plant a new variety of seeds in my 'kinder-garden' each year. I can't wait to wake up each day to help them grow, thrive, and bring out their natural beauty. Each unique flower makes our world so beautiful and colorful!"

—**Amy Westman**,
kindergarten teacher, Ohio

The Beautiful Game

Sometimes the lessons that transcend time are the ones that challenge us the most. These challenges can change our trajectories for the better if we let them. Interestingly enough, these are the same challenges we'd never choose to relive. Real learning can be really messy and hard, as this next story will reveal.

Soccer is a sport I've always loved. I played my entire childhood and was even voted one of our team's captains in high school. When I was eighteen years old, I was playing in a summer soccer league before college started. During one of our games, I injured a player.

I wish I could say his injury was the result of normal play, but it was not. I reacted very poorly to something, and with one swing of my forearm, I struck a player in the face with my wrist. On top of hurting another human being, this entire story is embarrassing because it is so contrary to how I was raised, what I believe, and how I live my life.

Some people might call this next part bad luck, but I call it divine intervention because it helped ensure I would learn an invaluable lesson relatively early in my life. The player I hit had a relative who was working as an attorney and a complaint was filed. I went on to accept responsibility in a court of law for the misdemeanor—and my family also reached out to the player to convey our heartfelt apologies. To this day, I'm reminded of my failure every time I complete a job application. Whether it was my first teaching job, first coaching job, or the two principal positions I've served (and am currently serving) in.

I don't share this humbling experience lightly; the learning I gleaned from it has been imprinted on my heart. Aside from the obvious lesson, there is an underlying mistake I'm hoping I can help others avoid. When it comes to learning and school, kids shouldn't have to wait for huge failures to learn lessons. Their paths should provide them countless opportunities to learn from smaller mistakes.

Small mistakes coupled with accountability and meaningful feedback can decrease the likelihood of harder lessons later on. I shared about my failure on the soccer field above, but you should know I was not a fighter in high school and rarely got into trouble. This might seem like great news,

Voices from the Field

"When I decided to let go of my fear, it opened up space to innovate. I was able to let go by deciding education is not about me but about the kids. It was a no-brainer! I just started taking risks, leaping, failing, and succeeding for kids. Through it all came growth and innovation."

—**Cori Orlando**,
elementary school
teacher, California

but the point is that we want kids to learn from lower-stakes failures and feedback from an early age.

Fortunately, public failures are not a prerequisite for transcendent learning. We can learn as much from the mistakes of other people as we can from our own. That said, we cannot and should not try to prevent students from making mistakes. Failure, in the right environment, can cement important learning and lead to long-term growth.

Schools that incorporate frequent opportunities for students to fail on lower-stakes work are actually investing in learning that lasts. When kids can overcome failures alongside supportive adults, they're better equipped to hold on to this learning when they encounter bigger barriers in higher-stakes arenas. This is not just a soccer thing; failure is something that should be in every classroom and school committed to transcendent learning.

Voices from the Field

"I strive to create an environment where deep learning takes place through the process of active and authentic questioning, a process that requires students to generate probing and clarifying questions based on their own curiosity and internal dialogue."

—**Carrie Lunetta**,
gifted and talented
teacher, Minnesota

I met with a teacher, for example, who shared that his students were struggling with a complex 3-D printing project. This was a higher-stakes project in that groups of students spent multiple class sessions to research and engineer a structure using advanced 3-D printing design software. The most important feedback some groups received didn't come until the very end of the unit when it was their turn to print their 3-D builds. (This is when some of the groups discovered they were unable to print their projects because of structural flaws that had gone undetected during the design process.)

What I appreciated most about hearing this teacher's story was how he had reflected on the problem and come up with a plan to help his students by incorporating more opportunities for lower-stakes failures in future lessons. He determined that providing students opportunities to "fail small" would provide scaffolding so their culminating projects were more successful. He could have easily concluded he needed to handle the final 3-D printing himself or discontinued allowing students to create these major builds. I love the fact that he did not resign to lowering expectations or look for ways to remove failure from the process.

When schools (or parents) try to remove the possibility of failure altogether, they limit the amount of longer-term learning that's occurring. Students of all ages need opportunities to make mistakes, generate alternate solutions, and wrestle with questions that don't necessarily have a right answer. Providing them these opportunities is an intentional investment in learning that lasts.

──────PUTTING IT INTO PRACTICE──────

You've probably heard of the term Return on Investment (ROI) before. ROI refers to the net profit an investor makes after factoring in the initial expenses. The significant investment educators make in students' health, safety, welfare, and long-term learning makes the term ROI seem somewhat shallow, so I'm going to invite us to identify an Act of Intentionality (AOI) instead. Your AOI doesn't need to be time-consuming or public. Small acts of intentionality done faithfully over time are what the core of our calling is really about.

I've presented several different ideas for being intentional about transcendent learning throughout this chapter, but feel free to try something that's more meaningful to you. Here are some additional ideas to help move toward transcendent learning by practicing an AOI on a daily basis:

1. Send one communication each day thanking a colleague for something specific, such as inspiring you to build deeper relationships with students or helping you with an idea to update your pedagogy.

2. Start a student leadership lunch bunch. An amazing teacher in our school does this by taking time each week to understand students' identities, which elevates our school's capacity to do the same.

3. Search for students who might be feeling invisible or undervalued in your class or school. Get to know them on a deeper level and look for opportunities to include them in meaningful ways.

Creating Conversation and Community

There aren't too many things I love more than hearing other people's progress on some of the same things I'm grappling with. Consider this an open invitation to share more about the intentional steps you're taking toward facilitating learning that lasts.

1. How would you explain the moral foundation of teaching to a parent (like Liz) who might be looking for assurances her child's identity is known and valued?

2. As you think about the concept of transcendent learning, how will you provide more safe, supported, and scaffolded opportunities to learn through small failures?

3. What evidence do you have that all of the learners you serve are experiencing a sense of belonging?

#ReclaimingOurCalling

Resources

1. Hammond, Zaretta L., *Culturally Responsive Teaching and the Brain* (Thousand Oaks, CA: Corwin, 2015).

2. Gonzales, Jennifer, "Culturally Responsive Teaching: 4 Misconceptions," *Cult of Pedagogy*, Sept. 10, 2017, cultofpedagogy. com/culturally-responsive-misconceptions.

3. Hammond, Zaretta, "3 Tips to Make Any Lesson More Culturally Responsive," *Cult of Pedagogy*, April 1, 2015, cultofpedagogy.com/ culturally-responsive-teaching-strategies.

PASSION II

The Heart
of Education

CHAPTER 4

Tattoos and Umbrellas

Backstory

The *heart* is where the thunder stirs. It is one of the most powerful forces in education, but tapping into the power of the heart is not always easy. This chapter will help you let go of the things that may be holding your heart back. In doing so, you'll be creating space for your heart to work.

WHAT DO YOU NEED TO LET GO OF TO CREATE MORE SPACE FOR YOUR HEART TO WORK?

Joey Forrest

Joey had his share of ups and downs while growing up. I was probably too hard on him when I highlighted his epic finish-line flop at his first track meet. If Joey were sitting next to me now, he'd be sure to mention he went on to earn "All Conference" honors as a sophomore on the varsity track team.

Those mini-seizures I mentioned earlier also turned out okay. Technically speaking, Joey had Tourette Syndrome (TS), not mini-seizures. Our class learned this after that whole-class talk. After that, everyone was a little more understanding of him.

Joey didn't talk much about his TS. About the only thing he ever said was he didn't have the kind of TS that is sensationalized on daytime television shows. Maybe you've seen the talk shows featuring kids inexplicably yelling out swear words? That definitely wasn't Joey.

Joey's tics were mainly facial twitches. He could explain this better, but the reason I brought this up is Joey felt like everyone saw him for his TS and not some of the good things he could do. It's true some people couldn't see past Joey's tics, but these were usually the same people who had no clue he took enrichment classes or that he was faster than most other kids at recess.

I know a lot of kids have it worse than Joey, and that's the whole point. When we're looking for deficits, we'll find them. When we search for strengths, we find those too. What we look for, we tend to find.

Kenny Mauer

Unfortunately, Kenny only looked for the worst in Joey and always seemed to find it—whether it was there or not.

Kenny had a name for Joey. I'll never forget it, but I'll never repeat it either. It was a soul-sucking name no middle schooler should have to hear. Once Kenny started using it, a couple other kids followed suit for the better part of a year. Of course, none of our teachers ever heard Kenny when he was destroying Joey with this name. I heard it, though.

That despicable name came out so casually, it was as if Kenny didn't know he knocked the wind out of Joey with those words. One thing is for sure: Kenny had a way of reminding a person who they weren't.

This is one reason I feel so strongly about searching for students' strengths and helping them see the strengths in themselves. For some students, school has become more about identifying weaknesses than anything else. For these students, school is similar to hanging out with Kenny Mauer five days a week.

I'm not naive enough to believe identifying areas students can improve is a bad thing. But when intervention and deficit-driven thinking start to suck the joy out of school, we've done a disservice to learning. Letting go of deficit-driven thinking is one thing we can do to create space for the heart to grow in schools. This is probably a good time to reflect upon some of the other things we're holding on to. Things that might be holding us back.

Try This!

Think about some of the strategies used to identify when a student is struggling. Try to jot down as many of the tools, tests, and types of formative assessment you use in one minute or less; next, start a second list and jot down all the ways you intentionally seek out student strengths. Reflect on how balanced (or imbalanced) your approach is and how you might try partnering with parents to shift the focus.

The Umbrellas We Carry

If you read the prologue to this book, you'll recall a ridiculous story about a borrowed beer umbrella. After I told my wife about that train wreck, she blessed me with a beautiful new umbrella big enough to keep a person dry in a tsunami. (This is one of many reasons I don't deserve her.)

On the first day of school the following year, I popped open my new umbrella to counter a light mist. As our community converged on our school parking lot, I spotted a student who needed help with her shoelaces. I set my new umbrella aside and walked toward her.

After greeting a few additional families, I headed back to my umbrella. There was just one problem: It was gone.

I searched the surrounding area and looked in our school's lost and found. Nothing.

I then did what any diligent principal would do: I reviewed some security footage and came to the conclusion my umbrella may have been more than misplaced. Frustrated at what I had just observed, I reached out to a good friend later that same evening to talk through my missing umbrella issue. He must have sensed how frustrated I was because the following week a replacement umbrella arrived in the mail.

Voices from the Field

"My students have always thought of me as a joyful teacher and leader, but there was a time in my life and career when I lost my way. I had switched to teaching middle school and also had my baby boy, two things I didn't have a blueprint for. I eventually let go of the idea that my circumstances controlled my joy. From that moment on, I found joy in the journey and started spreading joy to other teachers (just like I had done with my students)."

—Akilah Ellison, school administrator, Virginia

I was so intent to hang on to his thoughtful gift that I painted my initials on the top of the replacement umbrella in *huge* white letters. (Our school is in a suburb of Minneapolis, and I'm fairly certain anyone flying out of MSP while I was outside on bus duty would have seen these big bright letters from thirty thousand feet.)

A couple weeks later, I had the chance to work with some educators in Marin, California. The event venue was the storied Skywalker Ranch. This is the same place the legendary George Lucas worked for many years. As you might imagine, Lucas spared no expense when creating amenities on the ranch like a multi-story film research library, private *Star Wars* viewing theater, and even a small, man-made body of water appropriately referred to as Ewok Lake.

Before I left Skywalker Ranch, I purchased a Lightsaber umbrella in the small gift shop. You read that correctly. Lightsaber umbrella. In some ways, it was probably my Jedi destiny to replace my stolen umbrella with a Lightsaber umbrella.

You'd think *two* umbrellas later I would have let go of any resentment I had over my original umbrella being taken. I would have agreed with you until something terrible happened several months later. I was at a community event

Try This!

Try writing down one thing you'd like to let go of. This could be an unhelpful attitude about something, a bad habit, outdated practice, or even an excuse. Write yourself a reminder about this one thing so you can be intentional about truly releasing it. As difficult as it is to do, the act of letting go will create space for your heart to grow.

and had a short interaction with somebody that turned out to be rather embarrassing (for me). I'll get to that later in this chapter. The point I want to emphasize now is that we all carry things that hold us back.

Did You Know?

The context in which we work plays a role in what we can and can't let go of (e.g., curricular obligations). In many instances, however, we have more autonomy than we might think. One of the biggest challenges is actually deciding to let go. Most people do not instinctively let go of things.

The 1961 children's novel by Wilson Rawls, *Where the Red Fern Grows*, introduced readers to the notion that raccoons don't instinctively let go of things either. In the classic story, Billy's grandpa reveals a simple trap to catch the curious creatures: Drilling a small hole in a log or shallow container and placing a shiny object at the bottom presents an irresistible treasure. When a raccoon reaches through the hole to clench the shiny object, it is unable to remove its hand from the hole. The size of a raccoon's fist obviously increases when it is clenching an object, so the creature can't pull its hand back out the hole.

I definitely don't recommend this, but one of Joey's stepbrothers caught a raccoon in this manner when we were in middle school.

Voices from the Field

"Over the past few years, my thoughts have shifted from purely teaching content to empowering students to pursue endless possibilities. This shift in thinking has caused me to let go of the idea that I am the "giver of information" or that I need to remain rigidly connected to the curriculum. Now I'm able to walk alongside students and empower them to explore, create, and ask questions of themselves and others.

I am lucky to be in a school that allows me to take risks, try new things, and sometimes fail because it allows me to practice those same shifts alongside my students."

—Ginny Adams,
elementary school
teacher, Minnesota

He and I observed firsthand how this trap works. We also saw how vicious a trapped racoon can be.

As scary as that animal was, I've seen something even more frightening in schools. Just like trapped racoons, we (districts, schools, and individuals) hold on to unexamined routines and structures that stifle relationships, suppress potential, and overlook creativity. In doing so, we miss an opportunity to make school resonate with *all* learners.

A year ago or so, my wife told me something that gave me pause—and broke my heart a bit. She was driving our son, Finn, across town on an errand when out of the blue he commented, "There's that torture building I have to go to every day." Our son was only eight years old at the time, but his deep-seeded misgivings about a space that holds the potential to launch him into a lifetime of learning troubled us. Truth be told, our son would probably dislike any activity that requires him to get up early, but that didn't make his comment about his school sting any less.

If we want students to associate the same reverence for their schools as we do, we have got to stop clinging to practices and pedagogy they don't value. We need to rethink the things preventing students from falling in love with school.

Reimagining Relationships

Rethinking school will require us to confront the unexamined assumptions we carry with us. One example of this hit a little too close to home for our family. I'll never forget the year our school's Parent Teacher Association (PTA) approached me about starting a screen-free week at school.

I understood the goal of organizing a PTA event like this, but I had a few reservations. My thinking was the term "screen-free" might send mixed messages because all screen time is not equal. Students are using screens to create, collaborate, connect, and learn. These interactive experiences are distinctively different from watching television or brain melting for hours on end.

After dialoguing with our PTA about the different types of screen time, we were eager to partner together. We called our initiative "screen-aware" week, and my family participated by removing the large television from our family room. That was nine years ago, and we haven't brought the TV back inside!

Our family room is now filled with laughter, stories, reading, and wrestling (and piles of laundry). It's a beautiful thing. You could say our family created space for the heart of our home to shine. Once we let go, the space was filled with more intentional activities. We didn't gain any additional minutes in our day, but letting go allowed us to reclaim what we had all along.

I'm sure we could all identify something in our classroom or school that might be crowding out space where matters of the heart might otherwise reside. Identifying the things that inhibit our hearts can be difficult. Sometimes the best way to start is by listening.

Try This!

Identify one part of your classroom or school that might be getting in the way of building deeper relationships. Commit to critically examining something from your practice or environment you haven't questioned before. Rethink, rearrange, or reimagine something to create a change that will be meaningful to students.

Liz

What I'm about to share probably applies to every single conversation you'll ever have, but it was Liz who helped me understand how it also applies to parent-teacher conferences. The truth is, people are less interested in being impressed by you than you might think; they're much more interested in feeling heard.

I was the type of teacher who always overprepared for parent conferences, but since Liz knew our classroom and routine so well we were able to take an unconventional approach to conferences. Instead of starting her conference with a few pleasantries and then delving into the fancy score report I had generated, I started by really listening to her. She proceeded to share her hopes, dreams, and questions with me.

It's surprising how much we can learn about a person's inner motivations when we're actually listening for these signals. I've applied what I learned from Liz to a multitude of meetings and conversations over the years. One particularly challenging meeting with two parents stands out in my memory. Emotions were high and trust was low. I won't go into all the reasons for this, but it happens occasionally in schools.

I sat at the table alongside a teacher and the two parents, and we all knew we were at an impasse, but nobody expected what happened next: The teacher and I let go of our predetermined solutions and took time to really listen to the parents. When we shared, we made sure everything connected back to the signals and goals the parents had verbalized. This approach allowed us to be more purposeful in creating a path forward rooted in the hopes and dreams they had for their child. During the meeting, I used a template very similar to the Whole Learner Template on the next page. (See Figure 4.1.)

The template allowed us to take a step back from our agenda and created a space for the family to feel heard. The template on the next page reflects how almost every conversation I had with Liz seemed to flow, so in a way, I just jotted down how she entered into most conversations.

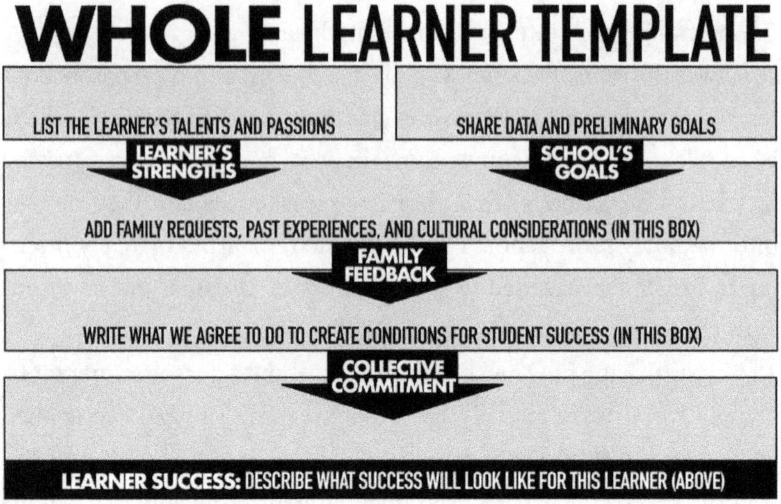

WHOLE LEARNER TEMPLATE

LIST THE LEARNER'S TALENTS AND PASSIONS	SHARE DATA AND PRELIMINARY GOALS
LEARNER'S STRENGTHS	**SCHOOL'S GOALS**

ADD FAMILY REQUESTS, PAST EXPERIENCES, AND CULTURAL CONSIDERATIONS (IN THIS BOX)

FAMILY FEEDBACK

WRITE WHAT WE AGREE TO DO TO CREATE CONDITIONS FOR STUDENT SUCCESS (IN THIS BOX)

COLLECTIVE COMMITMENT

LEARNER SUCCESS: DESCRIBE WHAT SUCCESS WILL LOOK LIKE FOR THIS LEARNER (ABOVE)

[Figure 4.1: Whole Learner Template]

Try This!

Try referencing the Whole Learner Template the next time you enter a parent-teacher conference or difficult conversation. You might be surprised at what you're able to accomplish when you pay more attention to where the other person's energy is coming from.

Parents are more receptive to the process when their family values and child's strengths are reflected in the proposed solution. As I alluded to earlier, this logic applies to every single conversation you'll ever have. When we listen to the language a person is using and look for the signals in what they're sharing, we usually have enough information to cocreate a new path forward together.

Overcoming Obstacles

I'm not naive enough to think difficult situations evaporate simply because we listen more. I can also confirm ignoring obstacles doesn't work. I remember my mom asking me to drive to the grocery store when I was about seventeen years old. After I picked up what she needed, I headed back to my car and chose to pull forward through the empty space ahead of me. My car unexpectedly crashed down on something so hard it felt as if I had been rear ended.

I quickly realized I had driven over one of those large, yellow concrete parking lot slabs. It took me a few seconds to decide what to do next, but I decided to keep pulling forward until my rear tires made it over the same obstacle. After my car thunderously crashed down a second time, I looked up and noticed an elderly woman standing in the parking lot staring at me in bewilderment. (I'm not going to lie; in that moment I felt like she was judging an entire generation of high school students based solely on my driving.)

The worst part about this story is what happened to my car. Driving over the concrete slab knocked my car's engine off its block, basically rendering the car useless since the repair would have cost more than the car was worth. Ignoring obstacles doesn't work in the grocery store parking lot, and it won't work in our schools either.

Let's be honest; some of the destructive practices associated with high-stakes testing have become huge obstacles to learning. Moving forward and pretending a problem doesn't exist makes as much sense as me ignoring that concrete barrier.

More Than a Number

Many educators are quick to point out how testing pressures have intensified over the past decade or so. You might be surprised to learn the push for greater accountability actually started in the 1970s when state legislatures began mandating tests requiring students to pass in order to advance to the next grade level—or to graduate. The purpose of these tests was to provide proof to legislators that students were learning.[1] These tests help us understand the degree to which a student has met curricular goals, but they do not come without a cost.

Earlier in this book, I shared a personal story about some curriculum-writing time I had been granted as a teacher. I can't help but think about what my students might have accomplished if I had used a more balanced approach to helping them achieve academically while also developing their gifts. If I had my first few years as a teacher to do over, I know exactly what I would do differently.

I'd get a tattoo.

I'm only partially kidding. It would need to be a temporary tattoo, but I'd try to make it one of those full-back tattoos because this is big. Here's what it would say:

WHAT WOULD SCHOOL LOOK LIKE IF WE HELD THE WHOLE LEARNER

IN THE SAME REGARD AS HIGH-STAKES TEST SCORES?

This question is something I continually reflect on now, but I didn't back then. (That's why a tattoo would have come in handy.) This question is also capable of guiding us toward creating more learner-driven schools.

The Umbrellas We Carry

As promised, I wanted to circle back to that embarrassing moment when I finally came face-to-face with the person who I thought took my umbrella. During our chance encounter at a community event, a flood of memories filled my mind.

I thought about the borrowed beer umbrella I had mistakenly used during bus duty. Of course, I couldn't help but remember the beautiful umbrella my wife had gifted me afterwards—the one that was taken. And who could forget the umbrella one of my friends sent me in the mail to help me move on, or the Star Wars lightsaber umbrella I scored while visiting Skywalker Ranch?

But when the flood of memories was over, I mostly thought about how rude it was that this person had taken my umbrella in the first place. Keep in mind I did not know this person, otherwise I probably would have handled the confrontation differently.

As much as I try to take the high road, I was still clinging to my desire for *umbrella justice*. When we first saw each other, we exchanged a few pleasantries and were very cordial. But here's the thing: I also found a way to artificially inject the word "umbrella" into our conversation. (It was not raining on this particular day, so I had no business bringing up the word.) I'm not sure the person even noticed my comment, but I am pretty sure my inability to let go was bringing *me* down. The person did not bite on my umbrella comment, and nobody has ever acknowledged taking that umbrella. I'm still not sure why it was taken. It could've been an honest mistake, but that seems unlikely.

Needless to say, I walked away from that community event without any semblance of umbrella justice. I actually felt pretty crummy for slipping the word *umbrella* into our conversation too. Back at home, I pledged to push past all the umbrella nonsense. I'm just glad I learned a lesson before I had an entire closet full of replacement umbrellas: You cannot invent the future if you refuse to let go of the past.

Here's the hard part: I knew my umbrella grudge was holding me back, and because of this, I had to let it go. I didn't get an apology from the person, and things were never reconciled. But it had become so abundantly clear that I needed to move on—for me—even if the other person wasn't part of the process. When we hold on to grudges, they often weigh us down while having no effect on the other person. When we carry this baggage around, we limit the capacity of our hearts to work.

> *You cannot invent the future if you refuse to let go of the past.*

There are other things we are subconsciously holding on to, and these things may be holding us (and others) back. Sometimes it's the baggage we're unaware of that can be even more damaging to everyone we're around.

All Means ALL

There are times we hold ill will toward a person (like my umbrella thief), and we know it. Knowing is half the battle when it comes to letting go of those negative feelings. We also need to open our hearts to the possibility that we may be unknowingly carrying preconceived thoughts about other people or groups of people. Before you think you're immune to holding hurtful assumptions about others, please consider the following:

I used to believe I didn't hold any bias until one day a student whom I knew and loved walked into my office. I had worked with the student plenty of times before in a behavioral-support capacity. We had spent some one-on-one time in our gym shooting baskets to decompress and even played together at recess. The student eventually transferred to another school, so I made a point of visiting him each year to see how he was doing. During one check-in he even shared an original rap song he had written.

Suffice it to say that we got along really well despite the fact that he had a harder time with other adults in his life. One day before he transferred out of our school, he walked into my office and wanted to read something to me. This was a pleasant surprise compared to many of our previous behavior-support encounters, so I was more than happy to listen.

Right before he started reading, I vaguely recall thinking he would need additional help from me to read. This was one of those subconscious notions I barely had time to acknowledge existed. I didn't even realize how unfair this fleeting thought was until he actually started reading.

And *read* he did.

He read fluently and above grade level. He read like no student I had heard read before. But "worst" of all, his reading far exceeded my expectations. I was left with the ugly reality that I had somehow been carrying a subconscious bias about him all along.

This experience prompted me to reflect on what other preconceived notions I might be carrying toward others. Letting go of this particular ugly umbrella required me to think critically about the assumption that had surfaced about this student. I had to acknowledge that just because a student receives behavior support doesn't mean he or she is anything short of a genius. I'm ashamed of this story, but mostly because I know how real that subconscious thought of mine was. I'm also thankful for the realization because it has challenged me to reflect on what other assumptions may be holding me—and my students—back.

Letting Go and Thinking Differently

Chances are good you're carrying something that is holding your heart back. It could be a habit, disposition, or unexamined assumption. I already shared how our family let go of the television in our family room during a screen-free week at school. Confronting our brain-melting routine helped us realize our viewing habits had been holding us back from deeper conversation.

The concept of letting go of the things holding our hearts back seems so simple; however, we know letting go in schools is not that easy. We are in a system designed to move forward without a well-defined process for expunging past initiatives, removing mandates, or discontinuing outdated curriculum. Maybe it's our sense of nostalgia that keeps us from letting go of things our students want or need us to release.

A large tile mural used to cover one of the walls in a hallway at school. It was created by students a long time ago. All of the students who had anything to do with the mural have graduated high school and probably have kids of their own by now. For some reason, we hung on to that antiquated art mural year after year. I used to think the mural was displayed because nobody was sure who might be offended if we removed it or replaced it with art created by our current students.

This past year, we removed the mural, but I was left wondering if my goal to avoid offending anyone connected to the old mural might have been a microcosm for other things we need to let go of. (I don't have to tell you we can only keep so many sacred cows in our system before it starts to feel a little claustrophobic.) Letting go is an opportunity to create space for the heart to work.

PUTTING IT INTO PRACTICE

The following activity will help you practice creating space for your heart. Start by writing down some of the unhelpful umbrellas you've been holding on to. I created a T-chart containing some things I'm wanting to let go of as well. (See Figure 4.2.)

Next to each of the items on your "Let Go" list, try writing a positive replacement or something that could grow if given the space to do so. For the purposes of this exercise, we're trying to describe how our hearts might respond when given the space to do so.

THINGS I COULD LET GO	THINGS MY HEART MIGHT EMBRACE
FEARFUL THINKING EXAMPLE: "I SHOULDN'T SAY ANYTHING OR TRY SOMETHING DIFFERENT BECAUSE I'M NOT SURE HOW IT WILL BE PERCEIVED."	**HUMBLE CONFIDENCE** EXAMPLE: "I CAN MAKE A DIFFERENCE OR TRY SOMETHING NEW AND I'LL BE OKAY IF THINGS DO NOT GO PERFECTLY."
RIGID THINKING EXAMPLE: "THIS IS HOW IT'S ALWAYS BEEN DONE AND IT SEEMS TO BE WORKING FOR MOST LEARNERS."	**LEARNER-CENTERED** EXAMPLE: "HOW MIGHT I LOOK AT THIS DIFFERENTLY SO EACH INDIVIDUAL LEARNER SUCCEEDS?"
ANTIQUATED APPROACH EXAMPLE: "I'LL STICK TO THE SAME TOOLS I'M COMFORTABLE WITH REGARDLESS OF OPTIONS AVAILABLE TO LEARNERS OUTSIDE OF SCHOOL."	**ITERATIVE APPROACH** EXAMPLE: "I'LL BUILD UPON MY EXPERIENCE AND CONTINUALLY TRY NEW TOOLS SO I REMAIN RELEVANT TO THOSE I SERVE."
COMPLIANCE-BASED EXAMPLE: "LEARNERS ARE EXPECTED TO MEET MY HIGH EXPECTATIONS, AND THEY WILL BE ENGAGED WHILE DOING SO."	**DRIVEN TO EMPOWER** EXAMPLE: "I WILL WORK TOWARDS DEVELOPING LEADERS WHO MAKE CHOICES ABOUT HOW THEY CREATE, CURATE, AND SHARE THEIR LEARNING."
FIXED MINDSET EXAMPLE: "I AM FRUSTRATED WITH THIS PERSON OR SITUATION AND PROBABLY WILL BE FOR A WHILE."	**EMPATHY AND GROWTH** EXAMPLE: "I CHOOSE TO MEET MY FRUSTRATIONS WITH A DESIRE TO LEARN MORE ABOUT THIS PERSON OR SITUATION."
PROFESSIONAL DEVELOPMENT EXAMPLE: "MY DEPARTMENT CHAIRPERSON, PRINCIPAL, OR SCHOOL DISTRICT IS RESPONSIBLE FOR PLANNING MY LEARNING AND I EXPECT IT TO BE GOOD."	**PROFESSIONAL LEARNING** EXAMPLE: "I SEE MYSELF AS A LEADER IN MY OWN LEARNING AND THE LEARNING OF OTHERS. I CAN POSITIVELY INFLUENCE HOW MY SCHOOL APPROACHES MEETINGS, TRAINING, AND MORE."

WHAT ARE YOUR LET GO AND EMBRACE EXAMPLES?

[Figure 4.2: Things I Could Let Go and Embrace]

Creating Conversation and Community

Several years ago, I knew very little about creating videos or podcasting, but I knew I couldn't provide relevant leadership to students and staff without letting go of my overreliance on some of the communication tools I was most comfortable with.

Once I let go of the way I had always done my newsletters, my heart had room to connect with others on a whole new level. We started creating video news segments with students and sharing them in the spaces their families were already interacting (e.g., social media, face-to-face, and at-school events). In addition to amplifying students' voices, I was able to build relationships with students by producing these podcasts together.

By letting go of some of the communication practices I was most comfortable with, I was able to implement new practices that effectively elevated the voices of students. This seemingly small act created another space for the heart of our school to gain traction. And that heart is our students.

1. When was the last time you and your colleagues had an authentic conversation about letting go to create space for the things you want to be more intentional about? (I can totally picture Mrs. MacLean asking me this first question.)
2. What is one umbrella you need to let go of to further empower the learners you serve?
3. If you were to design a tattoo quote representing your core beliefs about learning, what would it say?

#ReclaimingOurCalling

Resources

1. Popham, W. James, Assessment for Educational Leaders, Allyn & Bacon, 2006.

An Unofficial Chapter

TTTWRNs* and Lessons Learned

> *Teaching Things That Will Remain Nameless

If you're one of those people who leaves online reviews using Amazon, Goodreads, or another platform, I need to offer a *heartfelt* thanks (as well as a plea to forget what you're about to read). To make our little agreement official, I put together a quick waiver.

Your initials below signify this chapter on "Teaching Things That Will Remain Nameless" shall not be part of any online reviews or scholarly conversations for the book *Reclaiming Our Calling.*

X _____

DICTIONARY

TTTWRN

noun.

Abbreviation for: Teaching Things that Will Remain Nameless

Pronunciation: /tw-ern/

Alternate Spelling: twern

1. The things we know happen in schools, usually involving a semi-embarrassing moment. 2. Not conducive to scholarly conversation.

Word Origins: Classrooms everywhere

Used in a Sentence: The author shared a few TTTWRNs (twerns) and was banished from writing any books in the future.

Backstory

Teaching is hard, and anyone who has done it for any length of time understands what I'm talking about. As difficult as some of the work is, there are things that happen over the course of a school year only another educator could fully appreciate.

These things range from humorous to downright perplexing. And by the way, if you missed initialing the waiver on the previous page, please go back and sign it now. Seriously.

The Beautiful Game

Being a lifelong soccer player has its advantages, especially when trying to keep up with students outside during their recess time. But before I get to this *twern*, let me back up a second.

You can always tell when a principal attends a workshop or conference, because he or she comes back to school with a new initiative. (I didn't connect these dots until much later in my career, so now I try to be the kind of principal who is very intentional about the process our team uses to pursue new initiatives.)

I remember my very first teacher workshop week. I was fresh out of college and greener than green. Our principal sat everyone down in the cafeteria to kick off the school year with a review of the handbook. Over the course of the next two hours, we all noticed an emphasis on active supervision.

Our principal continued walking us through her expectations and gave several examples of what active supervision looked like at recess time. Active supervision meant we would walk the perimeter of the playground and monitor students while they played. We needed to be proactive. She emphasized how we should not become distracted or play games with students.

I took her words to heart, and for the next eight months, I tried to be a model teacher when it came to actively monitoring students. Toward the end of the year, I felt myself being drawn to a kickball game outside. Aside from soccer, kickball is one of my all-time favorite recess sports. I had resisted playing kickball with students during recess all school year long in the name of "active supervision," but this hadn't stopped my students from inviting me to play. Every. Day.

My students knew I was still a kid at heart, so even after eight months of diligently declining their invitations, they continued to ask. And their perseverance finally paid off.

"Just this one time," I said.

I took my place behind home plate, scanned the playground to ensure everyone was safe, and then readied myself for the sturdy rubber playground ball being pitched my way. The fact that I've played soccer my entire life definitely helps on the kickball field because I absolutely crushed that first pitch. In fact, it LAUNCHED off my foot!

It was a laser, but the trajectory was a little lower than what a homerun kick might look like. Actually, it was a lot lower. Before I could blink, it hit the pitcher square in the face. And the pitcher was only eight years old.

I was horrified.

My streak of safe-and-active supervision had come to a crashing halt. I sprinted toward the pitcher's mound while simultaneously scanning the playground again. Only this time I was checking to see what adults were around in case I needed help calling 9-1-1. (It was a pretty icky feeling.) After the nosebleed subsided, my student was all smiles—and she was totally okay. In fact, students started asking me to play more often, and it turned out our principal was on board too.

Lesson Learned: Active supervision is really important, but so is connecting with students outside the classroom. You do not need to play at a professional caliber or super-high intensity when joining students for recess kickball, checkers, or any other activity. Just the fact that you are on the field together is a win. (And never underestimate the impact of attending students' extracurricular activities.)

Mrs. MacLean

Even though I was eventually hired in the same district in which I student-taught, Mrs. MacLean and I didn't see each other as much as we had when I was in her classroom student teaching. The infrequency made any time our paths crossed seem extra special. I had been teaching for a few years, and we were fortunate to be able to reconnect during a graduate class each of us had enrolled in. I definitely appreciated the opportunity to work alongside Mrs. MacLean with a little more experience under my belt.

I'm not sure if I mentioned this yet, but I'm a bit of a germophobe. Mrs. MacLean got to see some of my germophobic tendencies first-hand when I was teaching with her. I still like to think my incessant hand washing worked in my favor most days, but that didn't stop her from giving me grief about it. Anyway, back to the graduate cohort we were in.

Our graduate instructors were always very family friendly and even allowed some of my colleagues to bring their newborn babies to our evening classes. This created a really neat atmosphere until one evening a colleague was passing her baby around during a break in class. With outstretched arms, she hoisted her child above the table where Mrs. MacLean and I were sitting, and another person reached across the table to complete the hand-off. Without missing a beat, the baby spit up when it was directly over *my* coffee cup.

You can't make this stuff up.

The precision of that baby's spit-up was impressive and revolting at the same time. I actually think I made my mentor prouder in that moment than my entire time teaching just by suppressing how grossed out I was. We all had a good laugh together—but I never used that mug again.

Lesson Learned: Experiencing the camaraderie and culture our graduate cohort enjoyed is an experience I'll always cherish. It impressed upon me the importance of making the workplace as family friendly as possible for all staff.

I'm proud to say a couple teacher-leaders in our school spear-headed an effort to help create a safe space for working mothers and staff with medical needs to privately tend to their needs in our school. I was more than happy to support the effort. Teachers often sacrifice their family time on behalf of students; the least we can do is work together to make the environment at school as supportive as possible.

More Than a Number

Some of the most heroic work being done in schools may never be reported by newspapers or reflected by the current assessment system. It should come as no surprise that some students are struggling with circumstances bigger than any high-stakes test. I remember the year I had a particular student experiencing circumstances no child should have to encounter. I'll call him Bryan.

Bryan joined our class partway through the year. His grandparents were caring for him while his parents were incarcerated. Despite having to carry a heavy burden, Bryan was one of the most tenderhearted kids I've ever taught. He also had a habit of running out of our classroom and hiding.

Suffice it to say that meeting Bryan's most basic needs was more important to me than some of the tasks we were expecting other students to do in school. My priorities included creating some semblance of safety and belonging for him. I tried to emphasize the reading and math too, but during the course of the year, I realized he needed me to be a different kind of teacher to him.

Eventually, the end of the school year came, and I was really interested to see how much Bryan had learned. I knew he had a nasty habit of speeding through tests, so I made sure to sit by him during one of our bigger computer-based assessments.

After Bryan had completed more than half his test, I found myself really eager to see the results. I had never seen him sustain his attention on anything academic for that long. I'm not sure why I remember this, but when Bryan reached question number thirty-one, I noticed another student in the room who needed help. I glanced back at Bryan, and he was still engaged with that particular test item.

I briskly stepped away from Bryan to help the other student. When I returned less than a minute later Bryan had finished the rest of his test. He had clicked through the *entire* thing!

I'm not sure how he was able to move his mouse through the remaining questions that quickly. Although we wouldn't be able to put much stock in those test results, I did see something in Bryan I hadn't observed before: He had developed a degree of trust and academic stamina that was not present when he first came to our class. It appeared as though the efforts of his grandparents and our team were making a difference. These are the efforts and stories a person probably won't read about in the newspaper. The heartfelt work teachers do to set students up for success in life doesn't always translate to higher test scores right away.

But this doesn't negate the importance of the work.

At the end of that school year, Bryan left our classroom knowing he was lovable and more equipped to love others. I also made sure he knew deep down that he was more than a number, and that is one of the most transcendent things we can impart upon students.

Lesson Learned: Teaching the whole learner is one of the noblest endeavors there is. If our only success metric is how a student performs on a particular test, we will develop a twisted perspective of learning. We need to stand firm on the moral foundation of teaching and help those who are newer to the profession do the same.

Joey Forrest

When we were kids, our Physical Education (PE) teacher always did an annual President's Fitness Challenge unit. Students who performed well even got a certificate that was signed (a.k.a. fake stamped) by the president. My memory is a little fuzzy on the whole program, but I remember one of our middle school sit-up tests like it was yesterday.

Our PE teacher knew better than to let Joey and me be partners, so she called him over. After she finished giving our class the directions, she knelt on Joey's shoes and started the timer.

Everything started out innocently enough. Half our class began doing as many sit-ups as possible while the rest of us looked on and tried as best we could to stabilize the feet of our partners as they lunged forward.

Joey was more competitive than any human being I have ever met. I've read that people with TS frequently have Obsessive-Compulsive Disorder (OCD) too. I'm thinking one of Joey's obsessions may have been "competing," but I don't really have any medical evidence to support my theory. Suffice it to say that Joey started by rattling off sit-ups as if our PE teacher was an Olympic scout. It was a sight to see.

And hear.

Each time Joey lunged forward he lost control of his digestive-system and made a very audible noise. I could tell he was extremely embarrassed because he actually stopped in the middle of the fitness test. That's when our PE teacher, who was also a master motivator, started yelling.

"Keep going, Joey, keep going!"

Joey resumed his impressive sit-up pace, as the uncontrollable sound effects accompanied each lunge forward. I don't remember how many sit-ups he actually rattled off in a minute, but I'd guess it was a staggering number if the audible indicator that snuck out each time was an accurate measure.

I'm guessing that for anybody else, this would have been their most embarrassing middle school moment. But since Joey had TS, I know he had bigger things to worry about than an upset stomach in PE class.

Lesson Learned: It's safe to say everyone has their struggles. It would have been really easy for our PE teacher to judge or abandon Joey in that moment. (I'm not sure I could have held his feet during the fireworks.) She was able to see past his issues and faithfully continued to encourage him. We'd do well to look past many of the faults and missteps of others too.

The Puck Stops Here

Most educators have experienced parent-teacher conference anxiety a time or two. Whether we need to deliver a delicate message, or a parent has demonstrated an inability to communicate humanely, seeing these meetings approaching on our conference schedule can create nerves in even the most experienced educators.

Jon Corippo is the Executive Director of CUE, but his twern came years ago when he was conducting parent-teacher conferences near Fresno, California. The story actually starts at a hockey game in Fresno just a few weeks before conferences.

When the puck dropped at center ice, Jon had no idea he'd be taking it home. This was one of his first hockey games ever, so you can imagine his surprise when the puck landed near his seat at one point in the game. When he reached down to retrieve it, he was shocked at how heavy it was.

The following day, Jon passed his souvenir around to his sixth graders who also marveled at how the puck felt more like a rock than a piece of sports equipment. The novelty of the new puck eventually wore off, and students transitioned back to their projects.

Shortly after that, a student whom we'll refer to as "Riley" started giving Jon a hard time about something from the back of the room. That's when inspiration struck. Coincidentally, Jon had received a realistic-looking foam hockey puck earlier that same school year.

He reached inside his desk while calling out Riley's name. He followed up with a "Knock it off, man," and winged the foam puck in the general direction of the unruly student. The foam puck did not travel very true through the air, and it immediately started curving toward Riley's head. That's when everything started to happen in slow motion. Riley's eyes began to bulge just as the puck hit him square on his forehead.

Wham!

Fully expecting the puck to be real, Riley went down to the ground thinking he had been knocked out or decapitated. Once he realized he was still conscious and experiencing no pain at all, he recovered the puck from the floor and exchanged some playful banter with his teacher.

The class enjoyed a laugh together, but Jon also realized his mighty hurl might not have been the smartest teaching move ever. A few days later, parent-teacher conference anxiety started to set in. Jon realized the hockey puck incident would likely come up.

When the day of Riley's conference arrived, Jon was half panicking as he waited for Riley's mom to mention the hockey-puck-to-the-face incident. Jon knew her from church, but she was laconic throughout the conference.

As the conference came to a close, Jon's self-talk started to sound something like *Oh my goodness, oh my goodness, oh my goodness,* and

That may not have been the best decision I ever made as a teacher; I hope it doesn't end it for me.

As the conference concluded, Riley's mom stood up to leave. That's when she looked at Jon and said, "About the hockey puck: Keep throwing toward him. He absolutely loves it, and it's one of the only reasons he loves coming to school."

Lesson Learned: First and foremost, don't chuck things in the classroom—even if you're not intending to hit anyone. Second, never underestimate the importance of connecting with kids in unique and unexpected ways. The small things we do to help kids know we see them and care about them could be the big things (in their eyes) that anchor their learning in a relationship.

Overcoming Obstacles

I suppose it's only fair I finish this unofficial chapter on a note that hits closer to home. I nearly needed to drop out when this twern happened in college. We were nearing the end of our first education course, and our "Philosophy of Education" papers were due.

With my paper proudly tucked in my backpack, I headed to class early enough so I could stop for lunch along the way. I scarfed down some fast food on campus and continued my trek to class. Before class officially started, several friends I had met were discussing their papers. I leaned in and listened, eager for my chance to contribute to the conversation.

I'm not sure what came over me, but I must have grown a little too comfortable over the course of the semester. At one point in the conversation, I tried to quietly relieve a little stomach pressure that had built up after lunch.

What happened next was devastating.

Everyone at my table looked at me and knew instantly something had gone terribly wrong. I left my backpack and "Philosophy of Education" paper at our table, and did a penguin shuffle to the nearest restroom.

I eventually had to decide if I'd return to class or save face and select a new major. I reluctantly tied my flannel shirt around my waist and humbly rejoined my classmates. Truthfully, the fact that I had left my backpack and paper in class gave me just the amount of courage I needed to slink back to my seat and rejoin my peers. I'm not sure how much I contributed the rest of that class period, but I learned a valuable lesson.

Lesson Learned: Teaching is family. With any family endeavor, there will be joys, laughs, and an occasional embarrassing moment. I hope the people you can lean on in these difficult times become evident to you, and that you are that person to your co-workers and students. It's an incredible calling, and sharing the ride with people you respect and love makes it all the more fulfilling.

CHAPTER 5

It Wasn't on My Radar

Backstory

Educators have hearts that lean toward seeing the best in people. We are forgiving, resilient, and pursue all that is good in our students. Yet somehow a data-driven slow creep has started to erode some really important priorities we share. This chapter will help us see some of our blind spots and fine-tune our radars so we don't lose sight of matters of the *heart*.

IF YOU WERE TO FOLLOW THE PRIORITIES OF YOUR HEART, WHAT WOULD YOU DO DIFFERENTLY IN YOUR SCHOOL TODAY, NEXT WEEK, AND NEXT YEAR?

Mrs. MacLean

Back when Mrs. Maclean and I were doing our co-teaching thing, we were able to cover a lot of ground together. She covered most of it, but over time I was able to chip in more and more. It wasn't uncommon for the main office to route an occasional parent-phone-call to her desk during the school day. I was even able to help with these calls occasionally. This worked out well until, one day, my help wasn't so helpful.

On that day, I answered the phone as students were lining up to transition to music class. The voice on the other end of the phone, as usual, was unfamiliar to me. It came from a parent asking to speak to his daughter, whom I'll call Gabby. I instinctively looked toward Mrs. MacLean for direction. She was busy, so I went through a quick mental checklist and determined that the timing of the call could work.

After a quick call, Gabby and I walked leisurely to catch up with the class who had started down the hallway. Mrs. MacLean was near the front of the line, so Gabby and I chatted near the back of the line. She was one of the younger students in our class, but what she lacked in maturity she made up for with emerging street smarts. It was a juxtaposition of sorts. Even at a young age, her positive outlook was being seasoned by some of the difficult life-lessons she learned through her parents' contentious divorce. Regardless of her challenging circumstances, Gabby was a true *light* in our class, pure and precious. I asked Gabby if her dad had called to confirm she was to take the bus home at the end of the day. What Gabby said next caught me completely off guard.

With zero hesitation, she said, "My dad just told me not to tell the judge he was doing drugs with his friends; otherwise, the judge will take me away."

I received her innocent words like a punch to the gut.

How could I have been so trusting? Receiving a phone call like *that* was not even on my radar. I made sure to update Mrs. MacLean on the call while our class was at music. From that day on, I vowed to do a better job creating a classroom where students had an opportunity to focus on learning.

My unassuming nature meant I wasn't exactly on guard against some of the outside influences that threaten the learning environment. As bad as missing some of these outside influences might sound, I think it's just as detrimental to neglect looking for the positives.

About a year ago, my wife handed me an invitation we had received to a taekwondo banquet for our oldest daughter. She had been nominated for a Junior Leadership Award. When we congratulated her for the nomination, we didn't sense much emotion in return.

She was stoic.

Our daughter has high-functioning autism, and it's possible her nomination may have meant more to my wife and me than it did to our daughter. I've always maintained the term "high-functioning" is an oxymoron when it's linked to autism and social interactions. This might be why my wife and I were overflowing with pride at the mere notion our daughter was excelling at something that involved other people (in a taekwondo-sorta way).

As weeks went by, the banquet fell off my radar until my wife informed me our daughter's taekwondo uniform was way too small. When we talked to our daughter about shopping for a new uniform, she matter-of-factly told us the *winner* of the Junior Leadership Award would receive a new uniform at the banquet; she wouldn't need us to buy a new uniform. (Did you catch what concerned us?)

About a week later, we followed up on the conversation with our daughter who again insisted she did not need us to buy her a new uniform, because it was the prize for the winner at the banquet. Fearing a meltdown of gigantic proportions, I decided to engage in what I call "expectation management."

First, I explained a large number of deserving kids had been nominated for the award. I also added some classic dad-psychology by joking, "I know you are going to think this sounds silly, but would we ever have a meltdown if our friend won the taekwondo award at the banquet?" I was relieved when she confirmed she would not have a meltdown, but I was convinced this whole nomination thing might go down in flames.

The day of the banquet arrived, and we conducted some final preparations like any good parents would do. (Basically, we made sure her handheld device was fully charged for the drive to and from the banquet.) When we arrived at the banquet, we were surprised at the number of people in attendance. It was larger than any wedding we had ever attended. The fact that I was a little overwhelmed by all the people at the banquet meant my daughter's social anxiety was probably through the roof.

My wife and I claimed a table and waited with our daughter while she squirmed in the dress we had bribed her to wear. When it came time for the Junior Leadership Award recipient to be announced, we held our breath and waited to hear the winner's name. And then we heard our daughter's name called.

Everyone heard her name. Because she had won. Our daughter.

She got out of her chair while simultaneously trying to put her shoes back on. I wasn't exactly sure why she had taken off her shoes in the first place, but looking back, it was just perfect. She made her way to the front of the banquet hall to collect the most beautiful, four-inch acrylic trophy I've ever seen.

When she came back to the table, I hugged her and took in the moment. Words can't explain the combination of pride, relief, and love I was feeling inside. It's a moment I'll never forget. And it was more than we had ever hoped for.

After the ceremony, a couple of my daughter's taekwondo friends and fellow nominees for the Junior Leadership Award approached her for a picture. My daughter's response was so unexpected that it brought me to tears. And that's quite the accomplishment since I was already crying. Later I will share how she responded, but I want to drive home this point: Sometimes our kids succeed in spite of us.

I'm not proud of this fact, but I praise God for it. If my own children's success was based solely on the quality of my parenting, we'd all be doomed. There will be times when we mess up, underestimate a child, or completely miss something important. The same is true of teaching.

I suppose we've all missed seeing certain traits in others around us, but let's be honest. The heart of education beats strongest when we recognize students' strengths and respond by fueling our students' passions and curiosities. Keeping relationships on our radar—in all we do—ensures we will see what our students are passionate about.

Try This!

Take a class roster and write one thing each of your students excels at next to their name. Put the list someplace where you'll look often (e.g., gradebook, screensaver, etc.). If you notice any names on your roster that are not paired with a talent, you know exactly what to do: Make time to discover those students' gifts! Use this list as a tool to inform instruction, planning, and parent communications.

Reimagining Relationships

Staff learning should be underpinned by relationships just like student learning, and relationships take time and nurturing. Our school recently brought in Donalyn Miller, one of America's leading voices on creating authentic reading experiences for students. We prioritized building relationships in the planning of our professional learning time—just like we'd do for our students. I'm going to share what we did to create a transcendent learning experience for staff, but I want to ask you to reflect on two questions as you read:

- In what ways were relationships prioritized in the professional development (PD) plans below?
- What evidence is there that our staff learning was transcendent?

When we initially scheduled Donalyn to speak, we booked her for an additional video connection in the weeks leading up to her visit. This check-in helped us begin developing a relationship with her that would eventually take our thinking further than a single day of PD ever could. When I was conducting my doctoral research, I identified ongoing and collegial learning experiences as vital, so our team prioritized creating a head-to-heart connection throughout Donalyn's PD.[1]

The day of her visit, we hit the ground running. I even heard stories of staff going to extraordinary efforts to ensure they didn't miss the PD. (Some staff called in favors with spouses to ensure they wouldn't need to stay home with sick children.) Their efforts were rewarded with an incredible day of conversation and learning. We planned some shared sessions in which all staff could participate regardless of their specialty area, but we also built some choice into the schedule, ensuring teachers could determine what sessions and times supported their specific needs.

Toward the end of our time together, we asked Donalyn for some recommended reading so we could build upon the momentum. She was happy to oblige, and we shared an article with staff after her visit. The fact that the article was recommended by somebody our staff had come to know and love didn't hurt anyone's interest in reading and rereading it either!

Our work with the concepts Donalyn introduced continues to this day. I recently attended a Scholastic Principal's Advisory Board meeting in Florida, and Donalyn approached me to offer a custom video greeting and follow-up to keep the connection with our team. She's also returning to our district this year.

In the weeks and months following her first visit, I observed teachers implementing new practices. When a couple teachers requested additional resources based on books Donalyn had mentioned, we added those to our staff lounge library. (See Figure 5.1.)

We've continued the learning in different PD sessions in the months following Donalyn's visit. In one session, staff met in small cross-grade groups and discussed the changes we were making to literacy practices. Teachers listened to how their colleagues were sharing their authentic reading lives with students and empowering students to do the same. These repeated check-ins have kept our literacy learning on the radar.

Try This!

The next time you have a meeting or PD day, try connecting with both the content and facilitators before, during, and after the actual workshop time, then be sure staff have a chance to do the same with one another. Of course, embedding choice and teacher voice into the planning and facilitation increases relevance and the likelihood of achieving learning that lasts.

[Figure 5.1: Staff Lounge Library]

Knowing the Learner

Earlier in this book, I shared a story about a teacher who was feeling frustrated with a student. I had a lot of empathy for this teacher because I had worked through a similar situation with a student and a follow-up phone call I made with her parent. I think I referred to this entire experience as a "career-jolting phone call" in Chapter Three. I want to circle back to this now because it illustrates how our blind spots directly impact the learners we serve—and what we can do about them.

Long story short, I had a student who would become extremely dysregulated, physical with staff, and insubordinate when she was frustrated. This frustration could have been the result of having to take turns during a game or not knowing an answer. My staff would call on me to provide support when she was fleeing the building or being destructive. I'm not proud to admit this, but most often my involvement meant the student would eventually be suspended from school. It felt like the only tool I had that made any difference.

That career-jolting phone call I mentioned was the result of one of these suspensions. The student's mom shared some insight with me during our call that continues to be some of the best learning I have ever experienced. After I informed the parent of the incident and resulting suspension, her heartfelt response to me stung more than I could have expected.

"I just wish you would have gotten to know her."

There is no substitute for knowing the learner.

The suspension stood, but I received her words like the gift they were. I thanked the parent for sharing, and we chatted a little more. We then hung up, and I made a decision to be better for the kids I serve. From that day forward, I made it my mission to get to know her daughter—and countless other kids—on a deeper level. Getting to know this parent's daughter included carving out intentional time together out of class to work on projects her daughter was passionate about. This included coding, building, and some work with our school drones. The difference was profound, and she was never in a situation where suspension from school was even an option again.

There is no substitute for knowing the learner.

Try This!

Think of a couple students who are really struggling. Aspire to know them better, but don't expect them to meet you where you are. Go to them. Spend time with them doing things they care about. You'll be surprised at the difference this can make over time.

The heart of our profession is not found in compliance-based exchanges. I still beat myself up for being so blind to this throughout my career. Starting a relationship can change a person's trajectory more than a school suspension or being excluded from class ever will. I'm just glad this parent had the heart to reveal my blind spot to me.

Did You Know?

Blind spots are a natural part of life. Not just figuratively, but in a physiological sense as well. We all have blind spots where our optic nerves meet our retinas. Chances are good you've never noticed your blind spot before, because your eyes work together to mitigate what you're missing.

Our optic nerves are basically bundles of fibers that carry messages from our eyes to our brain. There are no photoreceptor cells in the precise location where the optic nerve meets the retina; consequently, when light enters the eye, we cannot see it where the optic nerve connects to the retina. (See Figure 5.2.)

Here's a fun experiment you can do to prove to your students and colleagues they can't see everything. First, take a sheet of scratch paper and draw a small dot on the left side. Then, draw a hashtag on the right side. Next, pick up the paper and hold it an arm's length in front of you. I included a copy of this little experiment so you can do it without needing to tear apart any of the blank note pages in the back of the book. (See Figure 5.3.)

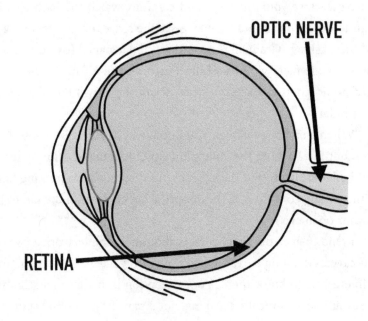

[Figure 5.2: Human Eye Diagram]

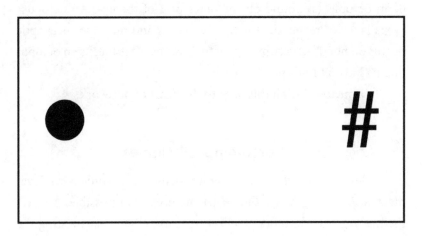

[Figure 5.3: Blindspot Experiment]

Now, close your right eye and carefully watch the hashtag with your left eye. You should be able to see the circle too, but focus solely on the hashtag. Gradually move the scratch paper (or your book) toward your face while carefully watching the hashtag. There will be a point when you see the circle disappear. It will literally fall off your radar![2]

When this happens, you will know where your blind spot is. If you continue to move the index card closer to your face the circle will suddenly reappear. (For the skeptics out there, this has nothing to do with how big your nose is; the disappearing circle is on the same side as your open eye.)

I tend to geek out on cool facts about how things work as well as any caveats that might exist. If you're anything like me, you might find it interesting to know there is one exception in nature that scientists are aware of: Technically speaking, not *everyone* has a blind spot.

The photoreceptors in an octopus's retina are found in the interior part of its eyeballs, but the cells that send messages to the brain of an octopus are found on the outer part of the eye. An octopus's eyeballs were created differently than yours and mine, so their optic nerves do not obstruct any part of their retina. This means an octopus doesn't have a blind spot![3]

It's time to bring all this back to the heart of our work.

Overcoming Obstacles

Unless you're an octopus, hyper-focusing on student achievement while trying to see the bigger picture is not possible. And yet the message to educators has been to make high-stakes testing the priority while somehow keeping other important skills on our radars.

Our systemic blind spot is causing transcendent learning to fall from our radars. If students leave us more aware of their deficiencies than their unique strengths, we will have done them a disservice. A hyper-focus on what kids can't do will lead to unforeseen challenges down the road.

My family recently went go-karting with some family friends. From the moment we met at the track, I was in all-out scouting mode, searching for the fastest kart. While waiting in line, I noticed one particular kart that appeared to be outperforming all the others. This would be the kart I would try to claim when it was our turn to take the track.

There was just one problem: My youngest daughter, Hope, was in front of me in line. I was worried she might notice the same kart I had my eyes on. We approached the employee who was collecting tickets, and I breathed a sigh of relief when Hope selected the kart in front of the one I wanted.

When the race started, I was surprised at how well my daughter fended off my attempts to pass her. This was one of her first times driving alone, and she defended the interior turns while keeping any outside passing attempts at bay extremely well. This cat-and-mouse game continued for several laps. Every time I saw her tiny head peek back, I was filled with fatherly pride.

She was completely dialed in and defending her lead like a pro.

When the track employee waved his flag, I knew I only had one lap left to make my move. As my daughter continued to swerve at all the right moments, I was beginning to think I may not get around her before the last lap ended. All of a sudden, Hope swerved straight toward a wall and crashed. (In all my years of go-karting, I don't ever recall seeing somebody hit the wall that hard or head-on.)

I was forced to make a split-second decision. I put my trust in the track employee's ability to perform CPR if needed and continued on to glory, finishing ahead of Hope. Thankfully she was okay, and we got back in line and compared racing notes while we waited. When I

Try This!

First, write down five key priorities you'd like to keep your radar focused on for the foreseeable future; for example, you might decide to focus on student voice, equity, technology integration, etc. (If you'd like a head start, go back to your "Big 3" from chapter one and build upon those.) Part two will come soon . . .

asked her what had happened, her answer was so obvious it surprised me. She said, "Dad, I was so focused on looking back to make sure you wouldn't pass me that I didn't see the wall in front of me."

Hope proved just how difficult it can be to balance several different priorities at one time. There is a two-part strategy I'll invite you to try that can help make the balance doable. The first step is listed to the left.

Letting Go and Thinking Differently

Keeping key priorities on your radar and revisiting them on a regular basis matters more than you might think. We don't see opportunities because they are there. We see them because we are looking for them.

> *We don't see opportunities because they are there. We see them because we are looking for them.*

In other words, we may miss things we're not looking for.

My sister and I took our fair share of road trips when we were younger. Our dad would always invent games to help my sister and me pass the time while traveling. One of the games we'd play involved searching for flags.

My dad would pay us a nickel for each flag we spotted from inside the car. This usually netted us a dollar or so during a two-hour road trip. Looking back, I can honestly say this was a stroke of parenting genius on my dad's part. I'd pay ten times what dad did for any semblance of harmony on the road trips my wife and I take with our kids.

I digress.

During one such road trip to a relative's house, my dad gave us an uncharacteristic "heads-up" as we headed up a steep hill. He told us just over the hill, on the left-hand side, was a campground loaded with flags. Needless to say, my sister and I glued our eyes on the left side of the road exactly where our dad had pointed.

We were completely dialed in and ready to cash in on every single flag at the campground. I was adding up those nickels before we even reached the crest of the hill. As we approached the top of the hill, we squinted into the horizon. Our dad pointed harder and we pressed our noses further into the glass. The campground never came.

Our resolve faded when we noticed our dad doing one of those suppressed grown-up giggles. We couldn't actually hear him laughing at first, but his entire body was convulsing with joy until he started making uncontrollable snorting noises. When he was finally able to talk, he confessed that while we were staring out the left side of the car, we had missed an auto dealership on the right side.

And you guessed it. The auto dealership probably had more flags on display than cars. We had been duped!

The moral of the story: Even when we are paying attention, we miss things if we're looking in the wrong direction. The same holds true for educators. Obviously, nobody tries to miss seeing important opportunities for students. At the same time, there's always an "opportunity cost" when we don't see something (or choose not to look for it).

David Culberhouse, a forward-thinking educator in Southern California, shared something with me that I haven't stopped thinking about. David and I were discussing two different countries and how each one tunes into different things when it comes to education. I'm probably going to oversimplify things, but I think you'll get the point.

Lawmakers in the United States have started introducing legislation directing schools to do more to teach media literacy. In effect, the bills being drafted are targeting the spread of "fake news" and designed to increase students' skills as critical consumers of online content. You can see the United States is making media literacy a key priority.

In contrast, David pointed out that China's state council identified courses related to artificial-intelligence (AI) as its key priority in primary and middle schools. This focus is intended to make China the major source for AI-related innovation in the world.

Can you imagine what either of these countries might accomplish in one year (or even ten years from now) by focusing their efforts on these key priorities? I'd imagine each country would be in a completely different stratosphere from where it is now—and equally as far from each other. I'm not making a value judgment on either country's key priority. I *am* suggesting the things on which we decide to focus will have consequences (good and bad) in the future.

Although my conversation with David uses examples at the state and policy level, similar decisions are playing out at the classroom level and in district offices everywhere. Once we recognize the urgency of deciding on the direction we're heading, we need to ensure the priorities we establish serve our students now and into their future.

I'm learning some of the things students need most from me might be completely out of my comfort zone or off my radar altogether. Chances are, you might be uncomfortable with some of the things students need you to learn as well. We can no longer ignore the fact that some of the tools and skills I might consider innovative (or optional) today could be essential to student success tomorrow.

You might be thinking it's hard enough to keep a group of students on your radar all day, let alone the education agenda for the United States and China. This is one reason why it's so important to identify your priorities. Priorities reveal our heart and set a purposeful path forward.

Voices from the Field

"Providing content and sending students to college does not necessarily future-proof them. We need to equip students with the skills to connect ideas in a rapidly changing world. Radar items like greater awareness, agility, and adaptability to the systems shifts rocking our societal pillars are critical. In this respect, the global workforce isn't looking for Einsteins as much as it is needing DaVincis."

—David Culberhouse, LCAP program manager, California

———PUTTING IT INTO PRACTICE———

Here's the second part of the exercise we started a few pages back. This activity will help you focus your heart on the important work and priorities ahead. It will also keep your radar sharp and mitigate your blind spots by tapping into the perspective of a trusted colleague.

I have broken the final part of this activity into a few steps, but don't let that scare you. Some of the steps are super quick, and the longer ones are worth your effort.

Start by revisiting the five key priorities (or radar items) you listed earlier in this chapter; next, add a short sentence for each of your five key priorities. The details you add will clarify what each item means to you. I went ahead and added a short sentence to the educational priorities from USA and China as an example for us to follow.

Media Literacy

Developing skills to evaluate the credibility and/or bias of an article or online source (USA).

Artificial Intelligence

Innovative and cross-disciplinary teaching focused on mastering machine intelligence and creating an internationally competitive workforce (China).

The next step is to attach a ranking to each of your five priorities. I'm sharing a list of five of my current priorities so you can see some of the things on my heart. (See Figure 5.4.) You'll notice I affixed a ranking to each of these radar items as well. I'm going to ask you to do the same to your list. Rank each priority on a scale of one to five, with one being your top priority.

MY FIVE **RADAR** ITEMS

TEACHING THE WHOLE LEARNER   1

UNLEASHING LEARNER-TALENT IN ALL ITS FORMS, AND SPARKING NEW CURIOSITIES WHERE THEY DID NOT PREVIOUSLY EXIST. DEVELOPING SKILLS SO STUDENTS CAN BE ADAPTIVE PROBLEM SOLVERS.

AN INSTITUTION OF EMPOWERED LEARNERS   4

LEARNERS SHOULD SEE EACH OTHER WORKING REALLY HARD TO LEARN (AND UNLEARN) SO THEIR NEEDS AND FUTURE IS SECURED.

CULTURALLY RESPONSIVE LEADERSHIP   2

BUILDING RELATIONSHIPS AND LEADING WORK AROUND CULTURE AND EQUITY SO ALL LEARNERS CAN PUT THEIR EMPATHY, EMOTIONAL INTELLIGENCE, AND CULTURAL COMPETENCE TO WORK.

PRIORITIZING AN INNOVATIVE AND LEARNER-   3 CENTERED PEDAGOGY

STAYING CURRENT WITH GLOBAL SIGNALS, INSTRUCTIONAL STRATEGIES, AND TOOLS CAPABLE OF EMPOWERING TODAY'S LEARNERS.

LEARNING THROUGH PLAY   5

REGARDLESS OF THE INTERVENTION SYSTEMS A SCHOOL HAS IN PLACE, ALL STUDENTS HAVE THE RIGHT TO PLAY, EXPERIENCE JOY, AND BE KIDS.

WHAT ARE **YOUR** RADAR ITEMS?

[Figure 5.4: My Five Radar Items]

Now comes the important part. Try not to shy away from this step: Schedule time with a trusted colleague to talk about your list. If you're lucky, your colleague will share a list with you as well. As you discuss your lists, try to notice things that might be missing. Look for things that surprise you about their rankings.

Talk about those things. Ask for feedback and suggestions to enhance your radar.

I'll admit there's a certain level of vulnerability in sharing your heart, passions, and rank-ordered priorities with another person. That's why the conversation is such an important part of this exercise. It allows you to reveal insights and provide a rationale for why you're currently seeing things the way you do. Feel free to add or amend your five radar items after conversing with your colleague.

> *What if every educator made a list of heartfelt passions and then asked a colleague to help enhance what's on their radar? How might our students benefit from this type of ongoing dialogue?*

Creating Conversation and Community

Identifying our radar items is one thing; keeping a sustained focus on several important priorities at once is another thing. This is why we included a trusted colleague in the conversation about our key priorities. Tapping into the wisdom and experience of others is a powerful way to confront our own blind spots. When we embrace our vulnerabilities, we open ourselves up to the possibility that we do not have to have all the answers.

1. What do you notice about the key priorities you've had the most success with over time?
2. What is one radar item you or your colleagues are wrestling with?
3. Mrs. MacLean has helped enhance my radar. Who has supported you, invested in you, and helped your heart see the learners you serve more clearly?

 #ReclaimingOurCalling

Resources

1. Gustafson, Brad R., "A Phenomenological Study of Professional Development in the Digital Age," *PQDT Open,* 2014, pqdtopen.proquest.com/pubnum/3648959.html.

2. "Eyes & Vision Science Lesson," *Home Science Tools,* hometrainingtools.com/a/blind-spot-science-project.

3. "The Blind Spot," *Sight Vision,* faculty.washington.edu/chudler/chvision.html.

PASSION III

The Mind
of Education

CHAPTER 6

Autopilot

Backstory

The *mind* of our profession is one of our greatest collective assets. Our thinking is informed by a vast amount of research and experience. All of this knowledge contributes to how we approach daily decisions in our classrooms and schools. At times, however, the brain's decision-making ability is hijacked by something I refer to as autopilot mode. In the pages that follow, we'll delve into six strategies to disrupt autopilot mode and the unhelpful scripts your mind might be running.

WHEN IS A TIME YOU FELT YOU MIGHT BE IN AUTOPILOT MODE?

Kenny Mauer

When it came to finding difficulties, Joey did not need any extra help. The deck of cards already seemed stacked against him. I think that's one reason Kenny seemed so cruel. He was always there to lend an unhelpful hand (or flick to the ear) when nobody was looking.

One day in high school Joey and I were eating lunch when two girls approached us in the cafeteria. I knew Joey *really* liked one of the girls. Her friend asked Joey a question, and he smiled a smile I hadn't seen before and nodded his head *yes*. It was too loud in the cafeteria to catch what she had asked, but after their exchange, the girls scuttled away to a different table.

Before they had even sat down, I leaned over and asked Joey what they had asked him. His shoulders shot up and he did one of his patented smile-shrugs and said, "I'm not sure; I couldn't hear her." I still don't understand how a person could have a conversation with somebody they had a crush on without being able to hear, but I gave Joey credit for at least trying. The problem was, I don't think the girls gave him the same credit.

When I looked back in their direction, they were seated with Kenny Mauer, and he appeared just as smitten by them as I knew my friend Joey was. You can probably guess how that whole situation ended for Joey.

He slunk down in his chair as if he had just lost the lottery. To make matters worse, it was a reoccurring lottery loss because the girls sat next to Kenny for several weeks after this encounter. I never had the courage to ask Joey's crush why she ended up sitting next to Kenny, but I did ask her best friend what the deal was, and you'll never guess what she said.

It turns out the question Joey had emphatically nodded his head to was pretty important. The girls had heard Joey liked a different classmate, so they had asked him, "Do you like Eva?" Joey's response in the affirmative sealed his fate and meant he'd lost a chance to date his real crush.

I still have my suspicions that Kenny engineered the rumor about Joey liking Eva—I wouldn't have put it past him. Before I get too off-track, I want us to pay attention to how Joey responded to the girls' original question—the question he never heard them ask.

His automatic response was to respond. You could argue he was so in love that he wasn't thinking clearly, and you'd probably be right. But I bet you'd be surprised at how often our brains respond to situations automatically.

Letting Go and Thinking Differently

I shared the story about getting rid of our family room television as part of a PTA screen-free week earlier in this book, and some people probably thought my family was from an alien species incapable of feeling the pain of no television.

I assure you, we felt the pain.

You haven't experienced first-world problems until you've quit watching home-improvement shows or twenty-four-hour sports coverage cold turkey! However heroic (or crazy) you thought we were for ditching our TV, nothing compares to what happened next: For nearly a month, I would wander mindlessly into the family room to stare at a blank wall for sports updates and home-improvement tips. All of this happened without me even thinking.

I had become so accustomed to sitting down in my favorite chair in the family room and staring in the direction of the TV that I continued to do so even after it was gone. I have to tell you: It felt kind of creepy to discover my routine was so cemented in my subconscious that I continually caught myself being drawn in by the gravitational pull of where our TV once sat. (I wish I were kidding.)

I already went over some of the benefits our family realized as a result of removing that TV, so I won't rehash those. But this story isn't really about a TV; it's about the unquestioned tendencies with which we approach different situations. It wasn't until I disrupted my routine that I discovered my own autopilot mode.

Voices from the Field

"I am driven to grow each day as a person and educator. To do this, I've been rebuilding my subconscious through positive mantras, listening to motivational videos, and reading books. The reason I'm trying to reprogram my subconscious is simple: The person who thinks he can is usually right."

—Martin Son,
middle school math
teacher, Illinois

Our brains are hardwired to make sense of things by looking for patterns and routines. This process typically plays out in the background of our neurological processing without us even knowing. It may sound simple, but the first strategy to short-circuiting your autopilot mode is to do something different each day to *disrupt your routine.*

Doing things differently is not the only way to get a handle on autopilot mode. Our school has had success by *iterating* annual practices. If you're anything like us, you expect certain traditions and seasonal processes to play out. Small modifications to annual activities and lessons make them more responsive to learners' needs.

We've even tried applying iteration to mundane budgeting practices. The first iteration started a few years ago when we appropriated a modest amount of money to support staff innovation using an additional line-item in the budget. We later iterated this approach by making the line-item for innovation more accessible to all staff. We started inviting teachers to submit a quick request via email. We called these requests "One-Sentence Grants" because they were easy to write and focused on improving all aspects of the student learning experience.

The energy behind the requests and new projects teachers are leading has been nothing short of inspiring. A subtle iteration to school budgeting processes has led to dramatically different outcomes. Imagine what might happen if we applied iteration to other aspects of our classrooms and schools.

> ## Try This!
>
> Change up one thing in your routine each day. You don't need to ditch your TV. You might start small by altering the route you take to work or be more intentional about connecting with different students and colleagues. You might try teaching from a different part of the room or introducing new tools to short-circuit autopilot mode.

All Means ALL

Our school district added kindergarten specialist time to our staffing model in all of our elementary schools. That addition led to kindergarten students receiving art instruction from an art specialist, music instruction from a music specialist, and so on. In the past, these activities were facilitated by students' homeroom teachers.

As exciting as the decision to offer kindergarten students more specialized instruction was, I fell into the trap of viewing it as a mundane moment. My thought process involved reusing the same specialist classes, structure, and schedule the other grade levels in our school had been using. It was a scheduling model that was already working.

After sleeping on the decision, I hit "pause" and realized our team had a real opportunity in front of us. Our district had determined the parameters all our elementary schools would follow, but within those parameters, each school had some options I hadn't considered. This led me to the realization this moment might not be as mundane as I had originally assumed.

I decided to collect additional input from our team and began talking with some of the teachers closest to the decision. We considered the skills we felt kindergarteners needed to learn today as well as the skills and experiences that would lead to transcendent learning. These conversations prompted us to implement a new "KinderCoding" experience during the school day. This was done at a time when very few schools were looking at coding classes, let alone teaching concepts of code in kindergarten. To outside observers, it may have appeared as if we had invented a new class, but what we really did was iterate our existing technology specialist time.

The second strategy to disrupt autopilot mode is to apply iteration to existing best practices. Some of the most meaningful changes we make involve applying innovation to what's already working.

Try This!

Try to improve upon something you are already doing well. Identify a lesson, unit, or school tradition and think of one small thing you might be able to refine to make the experience even more meaningful for participants.

Thanks to the groundbreaking work and collaboration by the teachers in our school, all kindergarten students now have opportunities to practice coding on a weekly basis as part of the core curriculum. Students still receive art, music, physical education, and technology, but they're also learning the language of computer coding. Let's be clear: This iteration was less about coding and more about learning that lasts. KinderCoding classes emphasize the value of risk-taking and building upon past mistakes. Students are learning to fail early and often as well as how to persevere using problem solving, collaboration, and divergent thinking. One of the things we're most proud of is the fact that many of the lessons in KinderCoding do not involve technology at all. Students will even start some lessons by programming their teacher (or classmates) using index cards and logic to determine the precise path a person will follow.

> **We can extend our impact as educators by looking at every mundane moment as an opportunity to iterate.**

Sometimes I sit back and reflect on what our students might be experiencing if we had simply settled for autopilot mode by replicating our existing specialist schedule and course offerings. Fortunately, a mundane decision turned into an opportunity for us to iterate using a pedagogy relevant to today's kindergarten students.

Did You Know?

Autopilot is a real thing. And I'm not even talking about autonomous vehicles, self-driving cars, and the like. It's estimated we spend nearly half our time in autopilot mode. While our brains effortlessly execute skills that were difficult to learn initially, our minds search for predictable routines. Whether we're walking down the stairs or typing on a touch-screen computer, we don't have to think about these things much, because a region in the brain known as the sensorimotor cortex assists in forming the tendencies eventually put on autopilot. There's a significant difference between the parts of the brain used when first learning a task compared to the parts of the brain used when a task becomes second nature. (See Figure 6.1.) Before tendencies are established, the prefrontal cortex communicates extensively with the striatum. Over time the communication with the prefrontal cortex is replaced by automated loops connecting the striatum to the sensorimotor cortex.[1] These loops allow us to complete mundane tasks without having to apply any effort at all. Welcome to autopilot mode!

The autopilot process reduces our need to overthink insignificant tasks, which allows us to focus our attention on more complex decisions. This is a good thing because it would be terribly inefficient if we had to concentrate to complete tasks that are mundane for most people (e.g., walking, typing, singing a familiar song). Unfortunately, the same process that makes our brains efficient also contributes to the formation of thought patterns and tendencies that can stifle learner-centered innovation.

The next time you approach a new situation, be aware of the fact that you might not be as open to new options as you think. (This is exactly what happened when I was considering replicating our existing specialist schedule when adding kindergarten specials.) Our brains are constantly looking for patterns and already filling in the blanks before we realize we may have made a decision by default.

Once we knew we wanted to be more intentional about applying iteration to our existing specialist time to make KinderCoding possible, another strategy came into play: *prototyping*. We used prototyping to push past constraints and envision new possibilities. When I use the term prototyping, I'm referring to the rapid creation of ideas or mental models.

Prototyping stops autopilot in its tracks. It reengages our prefrontal cortex and increases our ability to create plans capable of working within complex systems. Without the use of rapid prototyping, our brains could be left searching for patterns and return to that automated looping mode involving the sensorimotor cortex.

Educators tend to be incredibly adept at rapid prototyping. We often ask "How can I teach this lesson or skill differently?" From there we practice prototyping before formally creating lesson plans. Prototyping is enhanced when we are open to new ideas and communicate with others in our professional learning network.

THIS IS YOUR BRAIN ON **LEARNING**

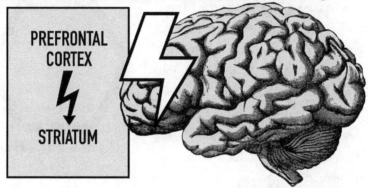

PREFRONTAL
CORTEX

STRIATUM

THIS IS YOUR BRAIN ON **AUTOPILOT**

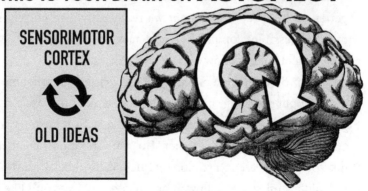

SENSORIMOTOR
CORTEX

OLD IDEAS

[Figure 6.1: Autopilot]

We've All Been There

I learned about the practice of prototyping from a forward-thinking technology integration specialist in the school district I'm currently serving in. Since then I developed a simple prototyping process that can be applied to virtually every level of decision making in a school system. Just for fun, take a few minutes to go through this process with me to see just how easy it can be. (This process will also illustrate the difference between iteration and prototyping.)

First, add a pattern or design to this hexagon. (See Figure 6.2.) Try to transform or camouflage the hexagon in some way—this is a form of iteration. You might morph it into a six-sided stop sign, for example. Spend at least two minutes adding details to your redesigned hexagon. After your two minutes are up, continue reading.

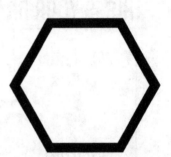

[Figure 6.2: Hexagon]

Think about how that hexagon might represent most learning activities or meetings you've ever been a part of. We can color in these experiences however we like, but we really only give ourselves one shot at successfully completing most tasks. Similarly, the tasks we assign students often follow a single path forward.

Rapid prototyping is a process that can disrupt autopilot mode by expanding our thinking. Look at the arrangement of hexagons (See Figure 6.3.) and redesign one of them just like before; next, try changing another hexagon. And another. This isn't about how creative you think you are (or aren't), so don't let deficit-thinking stop you. You could add a smiley face, a flower, or any other object you'd like to fill in the hexagons with. Try transforming as many of the hexagons as you can in the next two minutes.

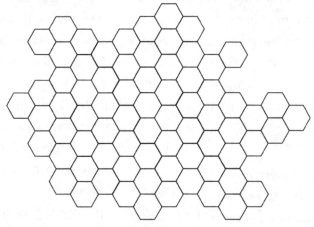

[Figure 6.3: Rapid Prototyping]

Pause for a minute and look at all the different ideas you filled those smaller hexagons with. The rapid-prototyping exercise above boosts creativity and is a great way to get more comfortable with the process of ideation. Instead of investing an entire two minutes into filling in the details on one single hexagon, we spent a comparable amount of time generating multiple ideas into several different hexagons.

By taking very small risks within the hexagons, we were practicing a strategy that can enhance our creative output in the classroom or any other role we're serving in. I remember being in a meeting with a team of teachers and discussing a student who was experiencing some significant challenges. These challenges, as they often do, were impacting everyone in a significant way. Suffice it to say that when the team sat down together, we knew we had our work cut out for us. Before we determined the specific interventions and supports we wanted to move forward on, we did some rapid prototyping together. We generated a long list of possible solutions before focusing on any one option for too long. This process allowed us to apply iteration to many different ideas put forward by colleagues too. When all was said and done, we had generated several solid options to consider.

Use this rapid prototyping strategy to stop autopilot mode and reshape your thinking. You can apply this strategy to the different decisions you and your team make throughout the day. It can be done independently through a quick and informal brainstorming process, or it could tap into the perspectives of multiple stakeholders.

Rapid prototyping is one of the quickest ways to generate new ideas; however, it's important to remember ideas that are missing student voice are not nearly as powerful. When our decisions are informed by the hopes and dreams of the learners we serve, autopilot mode doesn't stand a chance.

Try This!

Practice rapid prototyping in your current role. The next time you assign students a project or collaborate with colleagues on a challenge, try generating several different options before deciding to move forward on one specific solution. The more you practice prototyping, the more natural it will become.

Knowing the Learner

Learning more about students' families and interests outside of school is one of my favorite things to do; admittedly, I'm not always as intentional as I should be about carving out large chunks of time to practice being *learner driven*. This is one reason why I really look forward to holding events like Principal for a Day, and when the special day recently arrived, I felt ready. My young principal apprentice was dressed for the part too. He was even wearing a snazzy sport coat when he showed up in my office. I greeted him with a genuine smile and handshake before unknowingly slipping into autopilot mode. (I had done this Principal for a Day thing for several years and thought I had a pretty good grasp of what students tend to appreciate.)

After some casual conversation, I learned my young apprentice enjoyed playing soccer as much as I do. In between some fun activities like touring the school on three-wheeled trikes and participating in bonus physical education classes, we talked a lot about his soccer team and soccer statistics.

The conversation went beyond simple pleasantries, but our soccer chat was still pretty familiar; in fact, most of our morning activities followed a predictable routine up until recess and lunchtime. That's when my schedule opened up a bit, and my young apprentice and I had time to do some podcasting and video production work together.

I hadn't created my monthly BookTalk video yet, so that's where we started. The video we started collaborating on was for the book *Happy Dreamer* by Peter H. Reynolds. As my apprentice and I talked about the book's theme, we also shared our own passions and dreams. That's when I learned my young apprentice had a passion for magic tricks, and I could literally feel autopilot mode fade away. Sometimes the first hobby, sport, or talent we see in a student is not the thing they are most passionate about. The soccer conversation I had with my young apprentice was interesting, but it wasn't until the topic of magic came up that he came alive.

We found a way to weave his passion for magic into the opening hook in our BookTalk video, and when we visited classrooms for a read-aloud later in the day, we showcased his talent through a magic trick he shared. Seeing him shine during our time together was something special. (He even helped kick off our afterschool staff meeting with a few more magic tricks, and our team was all smiles.)

Sometimes students' passions are less evident than the sports jersey they're wearing or conversation topics we initiate; for example, it was amazing how we were able to move from small talk about soccer to a deeper connection in just a couple hours. Connecting to his passion and identity helped me to help him shine. (The fact that it took a children's picture book to open up this dialogue is not lost on me either.)

All of this relates to the fourth strategy and a magical way to make autopilot disappear. Each of us is called to be more learner driven.

Try This!

Get to know the learners you serve on a deeper level. Push past the urge to find common ground and get to know the dreams of individual students. After you've done this, look for opportunities to make learner-driven changes to your classroom or school.

More Than a Number

I want to circle back to something while we're still on the topic of knowing the learner. Earlier in this book, I encouraged us to hold the whole learner in the same high regard as test scores. (I may have even advocated for a tattoo along these lines.)

The rationale was that anyone who tries to reduce teaching to a single number or dimension doesn't understand the multitude of talents, needs, and dreams students bring to the classroom. Kids need opportunities to create, invent, learn, and unlearn without the system prioritizing a score over the actual learning experience. Students should stay curious because of school and not in spite of it.

Whether we like it or not, testing can have a way of sucking the curiosity out of learning if we're not intentional about placing the emphasis on learning that lasts. Achieving balance between getting to know the whole learner and administering assessments that inform academic instruction helps ensure our focus isn't shortsighted. I haven't heard too many people identify how we might be able to innovate within this particular box.

We already talked about inviting students to share one thing they'd like their teachers to know as a part of every assessment that's administered. Another way we could cultivate curiosity using assessments that are already in place is to invite students to respond to a writing prompt after completing a test.

- What is one thing you're curious about or wish you had more time to learn in school?
- What are the aspects of this class or school that really resonate with you?
- What is one thing about who you are that I might be missing?
- What is one thing you learned that wasn't on this test?

Imagine if we invited students to share a passion or idea that might help them learn better after every assessment they completed. How much better might we be able to serve the whole learner with this additional perspective?

Joey Forrest

I've already referenced collaborating with others and networking, but I want to talk about *seeking the perspective of others* as a strategy to disrupt autopilot. I'd assume everyone has been involved in an experience where two different people observed the same thing and walked away with distinctly different ideas about what had occurred (or what should have happened next).

By now you've probably surmised Joey and I became pretty close friends growing up. Whether we were playing Sonic the Hedgehog on Joey's Sega Genesis or building LEGO creations for hours on end, we always seemed to rotate through a few favorite activities. One of our favorite things to do was bike to a nearby park to play tennis together.

This was around the time Andre Agassi, one of the best tennis players ever to play the game, was dominating the tennis world. (He was also dominating this fanboy's heart, but that's another story.) In a time when most tennis players were wearing stark-white apparel, Agassi showed up to matches sporting unorthodox colors and an equally charismatic personality.

Joey probably thought I was a little obsessed when I would show up to our tennis matches wearing colorful headbands in homage to Agassi; still, Joey didn't seem to mind, because we were both fiery competitors. This competitive spirit served us well most of our childhood. Until one particular day we really locked horns.

I remember it like it was yesterday. Joey had just hit a drop shot over the net that had an insane amount of backspin. (I would never admit this to him, but it was probably the best slice I've ever seen on a tennis court.) I was standing at the baseline and didn't have a prayer of returning Joey's shot. And it turns out I didn't need to.

Somebody must have been smiling down on me, because after Joey's drop shot landed in front of me, it spun right back to his side of the court. No lie. Since neither of us had the official USTA rule book memorized, we did the next best thing: We launched into an epic debate about who should win the point.

It was true I had failed to actually return the shot, but why should I have to hit the ball back when it went back to Joey's side without needing my help, right?! Joey was incensed at the notion.

We ended up riding our bikes home unable to fathom what the other person could *possibly* be thinking. This is one possible outcome when two people start to fill in the blanks based upon their own background experiences. In the case of tennis, it's pretty easy to determine who is right because there *is* a rule book. (In case you were wondering, it turns out Joey was correct in that I would have needed to hit the ball before it bounced again in order to win the point.)

The rule book for our profession is less defined. We have many of the outcomes and curriculum we need to teach, but the process and pedagogy we use is largely up to us. We get to decide *how* we teach, learn, and lead. This is an exciting reality until we enter our classrooms and schools and encounter others who have different perspectives about how things should be done.

When we experience pushback and perspectives different from our own, we have a choice to make. We can either be open to learning about a different perspective, or we can cling to the scripts already looping in our minds. Figuratively speaking, the most growth-producing option is to keep your mind (and classroom door) open—don't ride your bike home in a huff.

Try This!

The next time you're looking to solve a problem, open your mind to additional ideas and perspectives. You might try checking one of the hashtags for this book, #ReclaimingOurCalling or #UndergroundBookClub, to identify educators who are on a similar journey. I'm always amazed at how much better my thinking is after it's informed by the experiences of others.

The fifth strategy to slice through autopilot mode is to seek additional perspective. The mind of this profession is too good a thing to waste, and learning from the experience of others is a powerful component of continuous improvement.

Liz

Just like we learn from others in the field, we also have an opportunity to glean important perspective from the parents with whom we work. I've already shared how Liz was gracious and truly cared about the overall success of the students in our classroom. Years of parenting informed her salt-of-the-earth perspectives.

One day Liz matter-of-factly stated, "You'll look at things differently when you're a parent." At that point in my career, I wasn't perceptive enough to recognize her words as an opportunity to learn more. I should have leaned into the statement and asked her to share more about what she meant. Her words seemed out of context at the time, and I still don't recall what I had done (or not done) to prompt them.

I'm guessing the friendly grin with which I responded felt like a signal to her that I had dismissed her words, but that's the opposite of what I had done. The truth is that I've been reflecting on what Liz shared for nearly two decades now, and I think I'm just starting to understand the wisdom. A parent's love cannot be confined by some of the artificial structures educators need to navigate. Where we see reading levels, budget codes, and different district departments, parents see their children's needs. The very best educators are able to see the perspectives of others while being able to navigate the system to meet the needs of their students. And the best way to understand somebody else's perspective is to be *fully present* when you're in the same spaces.

Reimagining Relationships

Several years ago, I was attending the International Society for Technology in Education (ISTE) conference. If you've never attended an ISTE conference, be prepared for lots of learning and even more people.

Lots and lots of people.

Some people are surprised when they learn I'm a closet introvert. I enjoy connecting with people, and I can be pretty passionate—and boisterous. But I prefer to recharge through reflection.

I don't remember the exact circumstances, but I vividly recall being in a bustling ISTE meeting space with several well-known educators, authors, and bloggers. I must have stumbled into that room by accident; although I recognized a few of the educators, they all seemed to know one another. I spent the first several minutes hanging back and making small talk with a couple educators whom I felt comfortable greeting.

A few minutes later, I noticed Jimmy Casas, a high school principal from Bettendorf, Iowa, enter the room. I had interacted with Jimmy via social media several times and thought I'd approach him to say hi. Jimmy's response was completely unexpected.

He dropped what he was doing, shook my hand, and initiated an authentic conversation that went on for what felt like twenty minutes or so. All the while, he was completely dialed in and didn't seem to notice the countless friends and faces that were more familiar to him in the ISTE crowd. He walked with me and talked as if we were the only two people in that room. Jimmy took time to ask questions and listened to every word I said. He didn't check his phone or try to rush our exchange. He was fully and completely present.

And I'm not even kidding about this next part.

It got to the point where I actually started feeling bad because he was *so* gracious. I started to feel like I needed to "ditch" him just so I wasn't keeping him from the friends who I knew wanted to see him. I gave him every opportunity to transition away from our conversation, but he wasn't interested in ending it. I don't share this story for

Try This!

Tuck your phone (or other potential distractions) into your pocket the next time you're in a meeting or talking with somebody. Even if your phone is not a distraction to you, seeing it may give others the impression that you're not fully invested in the moment.

any reason other than the impact it had on me.

We've talked a lot about capturing the potential in mundane moments throughout this chapter. We've also talked about pausing autopilot before making bigger decisions. I want to emphasize that no matter the size of the moment, it's important to be *in* it. To embrace it like Jimmy embraced our time together.

That brings us to the sixth and final strategy to interrupt autopilot mode. Be fully present. Make it a habit to be mindful of where you are and whom you're with. Chances are, you're probably right where you need to be.

I organized all six strategies into a single graphic. (See Figure 6.4.) The "Try This" challenges in this chapter were based upon the six strategies that follow. The mind of our profession can be a dynamic and learner-centered force when we short-circuit autopilot mode.

Back to Kenny Mauer

You might be wondering what strategy to try when you're up against your own Kenny Mauer. What if the situation (or person) you're facing feels like a long-term nemesis? What then?

I never finished that story from earlier in the book about Joey and me on the school bus. For most of the school year, our afternoon routine was a brutal testament to just how cruel (and covert) some kids can be. It seemed Kenny Mauer's favorite pastime had become flicking Joey's ear until it turned reddish purple. Every. Day.

6 STRATEGIES TO SHORT-CIRCUIT AUTOPILOT

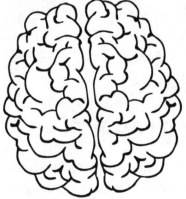

1. DISRUPT THE ROUTINE
2. APPLY ITERATION
3. TRY PROTOTYPING
4. LEARNER-DRIVEN THINKING
5. SEEK PERSPECTIVE
6. BE FULLY PRESENT

[Figure 6.4: Six Strategies to Short-Circuit Autopilot Thinking]

Until one afternoon when Joey disrupted the routine in an unexpected way.

My friend, red ear and all, got off the bus one stop early. He got off at *Kenny Mauer's* bus stop. And with one thunderous *CRACK*, he busted out of his shell and found his voice. He unapologetically explained to Kenny that his ear-flicking days were done. And in no uncertain terms, Kenny understood he would never flick anyone's ear again. Just to be clear, Joey accomplished this transformation using words and words alone.

As Joey's ear returned to a normal color, we eventually settled into a more uneventful routine on our afternoon bus rides home. But something was different about Joey. Things started to fall into place for him. Maybe that's because he was able to bring more of himself to different situations. I'm not sure.

What I am sure of is that Joey overcame a difficult situation. He disrupted a script and routine that had felt out of his control earlier in the school year. I'm not saying influencing challenging situations (or people) is as easy as having a conversation at a bus stop. Obviously every situation is different, and even the best strategy will fall on its face in the wrong context or tone. My point is that sometimes we have more influence than we might think. We just need to be brave enough to take the first step in a new direction.

PUTTING IT INTO PRACTICE

I already shared how our team starting using student podcasting as a tool to showcase students' passions while communicating with families. The podcasts supplanted our traditional newsletters, and the response was very positive.

As well-received as these video updates were by families, we recently iterated. I didn't want the fact that students had experienced success with the podcast format to mean the format would become the way we would always do things. Our school is moving forward on an innovative culture of literacy, and we want our communications to reflect that.

Last year we introduced the next iteration of our video news segments. Students started producing a literacy-themed podcast called "BookCast." The new format has been more student driven than I ever imagined it could be. We're still communicating with families, but now they're seeing authentic glimpses of our students' reading lives. We've even added guest cameos and student BookTalk DJs to the mix.

I encourage you to try iterating a current communication approach or strategy to short-circuit autopilot mode. Starting this week, try approaching a meeting, lesson, newsletter, or phone call differently. Your most mundane communication could be an opportunity to redefine your work.

Creating Conversation and Community

Remember those hexagons? I'd love to see how you approached that rapid prototyping practice activity if you're comfortable sharing. I posted a copy of the blank hexagon template along with an example I completed at BradGustafson.com in case you're interested. (Just look under the presentation resources on my website.) I'm also interested in hearing your thoughts below.

1. Given what you know about how our minds look for patterns, what are some additional strategies to disrupt unhelpful scripts we play in our minds? How might students like Joey benefit from explicit teaching in this area?

2. How would the culture of your classroom or school change if you practiced prototyping different options instead of advocating for a specific approach or single solution?

3. What is one practice you feel is a relative strength, and how might you iterate that practice to make it even more learner driven?

#RECLAIMINGOURCALLING

Resources

1. Ananthaswamy, Anil, "Break bad habits by hacking the autopilot in your brain," *NewScientist,* September 28, 2016, newscientist.com/article/mg23130930-700-break-bad-habits-by-hacking-the-autopilot-in-your-brain.

CHAPTER 7

Find Your Jelly

Backstory

I alluded to this in the last chapter: The majority of our time is experienced internally. Our *minds* reflect upon the decisions we make, just as we interpret the actions and motives of others. The same internal processes shape how we view talent. This chapter will have you thinking about strengths in a whole new way.

WHAT IS A STRENGTH OR PASSION YOU POSSESS THAT YOU HOPE OTHERS VALUE IN YOU?

Joey Forrest

As time passed, Joey and I traded in our LEGO sets and tennis racquets for drivers licenses and jobs. Joey even managed to tuck away enough money during high school to put a down payment on a fishing boat.

In college, his investment became our new favorite pastime. Despite the fact that we would spend countless hours together on his boat, Joey's jokes never got old. I can almost hear his voice now, correcting me when I would tell people we were going fishing. Joey would offer, "Well, I'm going fishing. Technically, Brad will be casting lures."

I found this line of thinking humorous and thought-provoking at the same time. The word "fishing" does imply fish are being caught. And yet, for Joey, the term fishing was clearly one that had to be earned. Being the competitor he was, Joey would invent friendly challenges to pass the time when the fish weren't biting for either of us. An example of this was the casting challenge he invented, which was essentially the fishing equivalent to doing trick shots in basketball or calling a home run in baseball. Joey would invent a funny name for a trick cast and then explain what he was aiming for. After that, he'd heave his heaviest lure toward the target.

I still remember the time Joey called out, "Half Mast" before explaining how he was going to hit the middle of a flagpole on shore. Our boat was bobbing quite some distance from that flagpole, so just the notion of casting that far seemed absurd. As I chuckled to myself about how fitting the name "Half Mast" was for the trick shot Joey was about to try, he snapped his rod and reel back behind his head and released it with a celebratory squeal. His fishing line immediately started spinning off his reel at a frenetic pace creating a high-pitched whizzing sound that reminded me of an angry hornet. I watched the scene play out, and I knew Joey had just launched one of the best casts

I had ever seen. We both cheered when we heard the loud metal ping of his lure as it bounced off the flagpole and straight back towards the lake!

Joey was at home on the water.

A funny thing happens when a person operates from a place of passion. Their passion spreads, and it elevates the work and thinking of others. This has certainly held true for Paolo (the student who wrote the foreword for this book) and it was true for Joey too. I know Joey's passion for fishing rubbed off on me because I fell in love with the sport (and trying trick-shot casts) as a result of the time we spent together.

The fact that we have the potential to powerfully and positively influence—and be influenced by—those around us is one reason why we can't afford to get lost in all the mundane processes that occupy so much of our professional lives. Call it what you want, but we've got to get serious about owning our own gifts and seeking out the passions in others.

I'm going to share another fishing story that ends tragically different from any of the adventures Joey and I ever had on the water together. Before you start reading, try to reflect on two questions:

- How are the people in the following story like you?
- How could they have better leveraged their own strengths or tapped into the strengths of others?

Did You Know?

Each January, the famous Tsukiji fish market in Japan auctions off the first bluefin tuna of the year. In recent years, the inaugural fish has weighed around 500 pounds and garnered between $70,000 and $1,760,000 at auction.[1]

While the world sushi market was not quite at the same level back in 1999, a very rare phenomenon occurred that year that had anyone with a boat tripping over themselves to get it in the water. It had been five decades since fishermen had reported tuna running so close to shore, and word spread fast. Against the advice of the Coast Guard, many people near Cape Cod, Massachusetts, launched their boats intent on landing a bluefin tuna for the first time.

The operative word being "landing."

The tuna were biting less than thirty miles from shore, but that wasn't the problem. As it turned out, catching a massive tuna and getting it into a boat requires a very specific skill set not possessed by the average person, and especially not by people who have never tried to catch a tuna before.

First, a nineteen-foot boat lost its battle with a tuna and was completely capsized. After that, a bigger boat became so swamped it fell to the same fate. Even a twenty-eight-foot boat was pulled underwater trying to land a six-hundred-pound tuna.[2] It was a train wreck on water.

The people in the story above were operating from their boats, but they were not operating from places of strength. Tuna fishing experts recommend specialized equipment, federal permits, and at least a thirty-foot boat. Had the boaters been more aware of their own strengths, or tapped into the strengths of those with the necessary skills and experience, the outcome could have been much different.

Tuna fishing is obviously very different from education.

I get that.

But I'm certain we can all think of examples when our efforts have "capsized" while trying to go at it alone without the help of those whose strengths supported the task at hand. Granted, we're not chasing giant bluefin or a quick payday. Our goals rest in the minds and potential of the learners we serve. Their long-term success is our ultimate prize. But it's unlikely they (or we) will fully realize that goal if we don't start thinking differently about strengths.

More Than a Number

Most of the tests we are tasked with administering measure a very specific skill set. In turn, we refer to students' scores on specific tests as their achievement level. Here's where things get perilous, albeit in a different way than the fishermen experienced: When educators are constantly told to increase student achievement without a mention of student talent, we can start to see kids as one-dimensional rather than multifaceted. When we are constantly asked to justify how taking time to develop students' creative confidence increases reading and math scores, we may begin to lose sight of the whole learner. Over time, messages requiring educators to focus solely on achievement contribute to destructive scripts that start to run in the background of our minds.

I'm going to share something that's kind of ugly but beautiful at the same time.

I'll get to the ugly part in a second; it's easier for me to start with the beautiful. One year I found out a student with whom we had been working with for several years was slated to switch schools due to a district boundary change.

This was a student who had experienced tremendous growth during her time with us. Although her growth had not fully translated to her test scores yet, she was in a much better place emotionally. When she had started with us, she wasn't capable of trusting staff, let alone attending class. Over time we got to know her heart and triggers, which allowed us to establish a deep relationship. That foundation slowly started to translate to academic achievement. It's not difficult to imagine just how concerned we were for her once we learned of the pending boundary change. As it turned out, the student ended up remaining in our school. That was the good news.

Here comes the ugly part.

During conversations about the looming boundary changes, this student's test scores crossed my mind (and not for altruistic reasons). I knew keeping her at our school could potentially impact the site data others use to judge our programming. I will share with absolute certainty this line of thinking did not flow from my heart, but rather from unhelpful scripts that had taken seed in my mind over the years.

Rest assured, we made the right choice for this student, but it's still unfortunate to think we serve in a system that potentially pits a child's test scores against a more complete version of who they might become. Think about that for a second.

Sharing this story now serves two important purposes: First, I hope acknowledging this type of thinking prevents similarly insidious scripts from taking root in my mind—or in yours. Secondly, I hope to highlight how my views of a student could have succumbed to systemic pressures. I'm starting to wonder if the problem with high-stakes testing resides in the way these tests can reduce living, breathing, human beings to data points if we're not careful.

Try This!

Pay close attention to how learners are referred to when educators are meeting over the next couple weeks. If you hear learners being referred to as "low, at-risk, reluctant, behavior problems, gifted and talented, special ed., etc." make a mental note. Most of these terms limit our understanding of students or emphasize their disability, label, or test scores over their identity. Try seeing the person first and let your language reflect it.

Test data should not be a judgment about the worth of a child (or teacher), but rather something that informs how we help them move forward. Meaningful assessment practices should serve as mile markers along a journey toward proficiency.

Our thinking determines the scripts we run in our minds, and those scripts influence our language. Our language becomes the narrative, and the narrative creates culture. If we want to work in a culture that helps us unlock the potential in all the students we serve, the language we use needs to reflect how we want to see students.

Knowing the Learner

So how do we start to change culture? Think about the last time you noticed a student or colleague's strengths. Picture the details around this encounter in your mind. Start by reflecting on what that person's specific strength was and how you responded.

Knowing the learner involves seeing strengths and talents. The more you practice this line of thinking or another internal script that might work better for you, the more natural it will become. Like any muscle, your mind's ability to see strengths will get stronger if you're intentional about developing it.

Try This!

Now that you have an example of a student or colleague's strength in your mind, try to fill in as many blanks as you can on the talent-seeking script on the next page. (See Figure 7.1.) You might not be able to complete more than a couple lines, but that's okay for your first run through.

TALENT-SEEKING
SCRIPT

SEE IT: _____

NOTICE THE STRENGTH OR TALENT

SAY IT: _____

EXPLICITLY ACKNOWLEDGE IT

SET IT FREE: _____

UNLEASH IT, NURTURE IT, AND LET OTHERS LEARN FROM IT

CELEBRATE IT: _____

WHY IS THE STRENGTH OR TALENT IMPORTANT?
WHO WOULD BE AN AUTHENTIC AUDIENCE FOR IT?

TRAIN YOUR BRAIN TO SEE TALENT

[Figure 7.1: Talent-Seeking Script]

Seeing Strengths

Our team sees strengths daily, and I love celebrating those strengths with them and our school community. When we are intentional about looking for others' strengths, we're able to create a more complete narrative about them. This is important for our colleagues, but it is vital to our ability to develop and celebrate the strengths in the learners we serve.

One of our teachers, for example, sent me an email indicating she had noticed a specific strength in a student. The teacher was looking for support to help cultivate a particular student's passion. The passion was related to computer programming, and after receiving the teacher's email, we connected with the student, the student's family, and our learning networks to determine how we would respond to the passion we had noticed. We all agreed learner ownership would be higher if the student was given the opportunity to build a computer from scratch prior to working on the actual programming, so our school made a relatively small investment to make this happen.

The student was allowed to work on this project during the day and after school, and when requested, we accommodated the student's desire to work on the computer at home.

The learning that came out of this effort did not stop with this student, however. This passion project sparked curiosity in other learners, and a funny thing started to happen: The student's classmates went from being curious onlookers to dedicated assistants. Seeing the strengths of their classmate caused some students to notice similar interests in themselves. The *jelly* started to spread! And it all started because one teacher saw a student's strength and determined to amplify it.

Most educators are very comfortable seeing the strengths of their students. Many of us, however, shy away from recognizing and sharing our own. In fact, the prevailing script running through most people's minds is to compare their relative weaknesses (or areas of average) to other people's strengths. We focus on our shortcomings and pay little attention to the very traits others admire in us.

This is a travesty of talent.

When we allow our minds to get stuck on all the reasons we are *not* equipped to accomplish a task, dream a dream, or contribute to a high-powered team, we will never measure up. Honestly, we would not allow our students to talk about themselves in the same way we sometimes think about ourselves. Fortunately, there is a powerful script we can employ to supplant self-doubt and unhealthy comparisons. Let me explain.

THE DONUT THEOREM

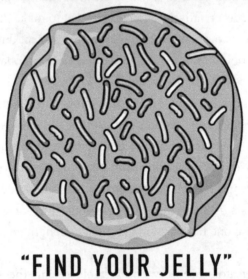

"FIND YOUR JELLY"

[Figure 7.2: The Donut Theorem – Find Your Jelly]

Analogous to Teaching

Some people talk about "passion," and others call it "flow." I've come to think of it as jelly—just like on the inside of a donut. By the end of this chapter, I hope I can convince you to find yours. (See Figure 7.2.)

You might be questioning my donut credentials to be positing such a theory; I assure you I'm well-versed in all things pastry. For starters, my grandparents owned a bakery for many years, so I consumed more than my fair share of donuts growing up. I've also participated in some donut-related activism. My first year of teaching, some co-workers tried to replace payday donuts with a fruit-and-yogurt alternative. After some bilateral negotiations, I'm proud to say "Donut Day" lived on.

Now that my street cred is fully established, let's dive into the Donut Theorem.

Just as the sweet center of a giant jelly-filled donut is confectionary treasure, our jelly represents our greatest gifts. Your jelly is exactly what you were called to share when you said "yes" to this incredible profession. Your jelly represents your passions, and these are the passions in which your geek flag should be firmly planted.

When we're doing something related to our jelly, time flies. When our work is fueled by our jelly, we jump higher, reach farther, and make a bigger difference. Our jelly is the stuff we love to do. As such, nobody else can be relied upon to find *your* jelly or infuse *your* work with it. We are solely responsible for seeing our own jelly and applying it to our work.

This has me thinking that if we all had X-ray donut vision right now, what jelly would others see in you?

[Figure 7.3: The Donut Theorem X-ray]

Of course, we'd see lots of crust. (See Figure 7.3.) The crust represents important traits many of us possess. These traits help us complete much of the work we're responsible for completing. The crust is

important and carries different nutritional value than the jelly. As important as your crust is, there's something deeper and more unique to you. That's your jelly, and you need to find it! The crust can taste pretty good, but it's always better with jelly.

I have been in education long enough to know educators are some of the humblest people on the planet, but I'm going to ask you to

Try This!

Turn to the notes section in the back of this book and look for the page with the donut on the top. Take one minute to list as many of your gifts, passions, and talents as you can. There is no wrong way to do this—as long as you take at least sixty seconds to write your Jelly List.

do the "Try This!" activity above anyway. Please resist the temptation to skip this part, and don't sell yourself short by trying to do this in the margin.

Here's where the theorem part comes into play: Whenever you, as a learner, are diving into a new task or project, it's important to *find your jelly*. Regardless of the task at hand, think about your strengths and strive to leverage those in the learning process. Your jelly represents your passions, curiosity, and strengths—the very things you should continue to develop. I added a gluten-free illustration of the Donut Theorem (See Figure 7.4.), but the bottom line is don't ever shy away from your jelly!

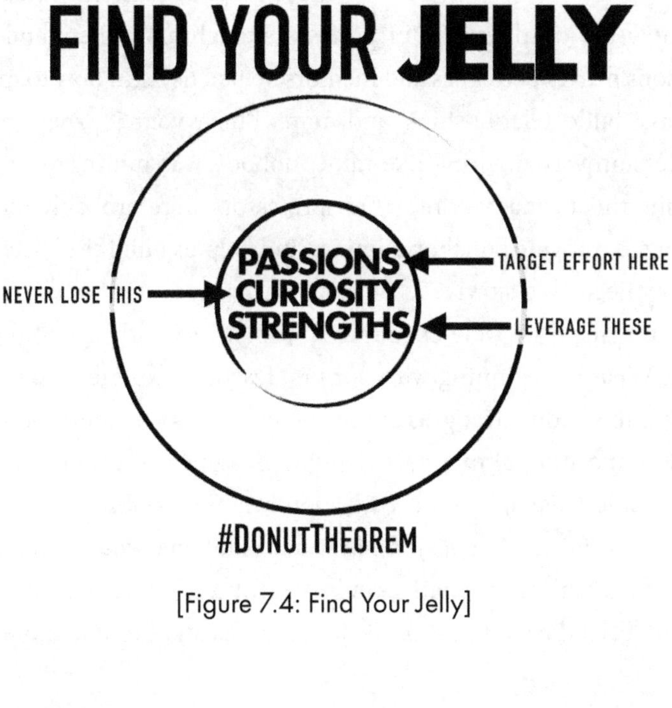

FIND YOUR **JELLY**

NEVER LOSE THIS ——▶ **PASSIONS CURIOSITY STRENGTHS** ◀—— TARGET EFFORT HERE

◀—— LEVERAGE THESE

#DONUTTHEOREM

[Figure 7.4: Find Your Jelly]

Voices from the Field

"As a mom, I want my kids to have experiences in school that build on their strengths and interests to empower them to find their place in the world, and as an educator, I am passionate about making sure we do the same for all kids."

—Dr. Katie Martin,
director of District
Leadership, California

Most of us have been conditioned to accept tasks as they are presented. From the moment we entered school many years ago, we were told what to do, when to do it, and given very little latitude on how it should be done. There may have been moments we were provided some degree of choice, but the choices weren't always super meaningful.

The same holds true in many colleges and teacher preparation programs. The learning curve to become an educator is steep, and most of us acknowledged early on there was a lot to learn. Our professors taught us content and skills. Various field experiences and mentors helped us learn how to manage a class, build relationships, and more. But if your journey into the profession was anything like mine, nobody was mining your talent during this formative time. (Our professors were probably too busy trying to mitigate our shortcomings and help us build the basic proficiency needed to survive in a classroom.)

Imagine if we were encouraged from a very early age to find our jelly. What if, beginning with our first learning experiences, we were taught to see our strengths so we could address our shortcomings in a more meaningful manner? Can you imagine the cumulative effect this would have had on how we approach our work now? Education would be filled with *jelly finders,* and students would understand how their unique strengths could benefit any situation. Best of all, they'd learn the strengths of their classmates and become more adept at seeking out those strengths to enhance their own learning.

The idea of seeking out passions may seem somewhat unrealistic when you consider everything else you're responsible for accomplishing. I would argue this makes it even more important to pair your passions with at least one thing you do every day. Finding your jelly is an important step in reclaiming our calling—and in doing so, you might just start a movement that supports others who see value in your vision!

When we said *yes* to changing the world through education, nobody expected us to say *no* to our strengths and passions. Find your jelly! It's in you, and it should be your gift to the world. Start leveraging your passions and strengths regardless of whether others see those same strengths in you yet. Don't spend another day chomping around the crust of your donut or waiting for somebody else to pass you the jelly. Regardless of the task ahead of you, try to take a bite that includes jelly every time.

Voices from the Field

"I'm passionate about the power of deeper connections between and among stakeholders as a means of moving education forward. I continue to advocate for professional learning opportunities focused on the power of connection. When I started EduMatch, I was a classroom teacher who worked to connect my students to each other and a global community of learners, but my new role has me connecting adult learners."

—Dr. Sarah Thomas, regional technology coordinator and founder/CEO of EduMatch, Maryland

Mrs. MacLean

By now, you know Mrs. Maclean was a gifted educator in every sense of the word. I bet you could even venture a guess as to what her "jelly" was. She had a passion for relationships, loved riddles, and always found a way to infuse literacy into whatever she was teaching. These were definite strengths, but I think Mrs. MacLean had an even greater gift. She seemed to derive joy from empowering others to own their talents and share them with the world. Her classroom was like a giant jelly-finding factory. And because she knew her learners so well, they were always building on their passions while connecting to new learning and content. There's a reason passion for learning was so contagious in her classroom.

Passion is a lot like the brightly colored, viscous jelly that oozed out of the donuts my grandpa used to make in his bakery. When that jelly came into contact with my hand—or the front of my T-shirts—it

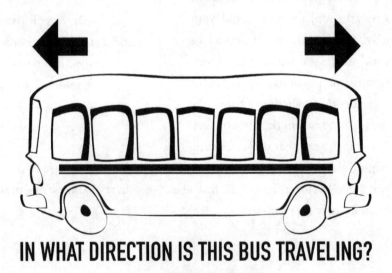

IN WHAT DIRECTION IS THIS BUS TRAVELING?

Image: Adapted from a popular logic puzzle

[Figure 7.5: What Direction Is This Bus Traveling?[3]]

was nearly impossible to wipe off. That's how sticky the sweet, gooey stuff was!

The same can be said about learners' passions.

That's why Mrs. MacLean relentlessly pursued her students' passions while unabashedly owning hers. It was a beautiful, sticky combination. In honor of my friend and mentor, I'm going to share one last brain teaser with you.

Take a look at the school bus. (See Figure 7.5.) See if you can determine the direction the bus is traveling. Sometimes I share a similar image at conferences, and I'm always amused at the responses it elicits. Some people venture a 50/50 guess and yell out "Right" or "Left." There's always one in the crowd who takes a more practical approach by uttering, "Forward." (Spoiler Alert: The actual answer relies upon some inferencing related to where the school bus door is.)

In addition to this being a hat-tip to Mrs. MacLean, I share this riddle because it reminds me of the importance of choosing the path to best meet the needs of the learners we serve. A student's jelly should always be considered prior to taking a lesson or learning experience in the direction we want it to go.

When I was teaching with Mrs. MacLean, we had a student who had a learning disability. While most people might have looked at the student and immediately noticed her limitations, Mrs. MacLean always started by celebrating the student's jelly. This made every encounter they had special.

Their greetings were more like two long-lost friends reuniting than anything else. The student happened to have a fascination with a popular cartoon called *My Little Pony*, and Mrs. MacLean always found a way to ask her about the cartoon. This made the student beam, and I swear Mrs. MacLean was watching the cartoon at home just to be able to connect with the student. It was powerful to see.

This shouldn't come as a surprise, but that student excelled in Mrs. MacLean's class like no other. And our students all took note. They figured if their teacher could manage to celebrate the student's passion every time she saw her, the least they could do was follow suit.

I'll never forget the field trip we went on that same school year. The permission slips Mrs. MacLean sent home outlined how we'd spend the bulk of our time at the Science Museum of Minnesota and then be making a stop for lunch near a big-box electronics retailer on the way back to school. The pit stop on the way home may sound a bit odd, but keep in mind, Mrs. MacLean was one of the most purposeful people you'll ever meet.

I don't know how she did it, but I literally teared up when we stepped foot into the electronics store on the drive back to school. The wall-to-wall television display was filled with colorful cartoon ponies. In that moment, our entire class experienced the incredible lengths their teacher would go to find their jelly. Mrs. MacLean taught us... seeing strengths and celebrating passions is one of the fastest ways to form a head-to-heart connection.

> *Mrs. MacLean taught us...seeing strengths and celebrating passions is one of the fastest ways to form a head-to-heart connection.*

When we own our passions and look for our students' passions, we begin to see the sweet spot where Mrs. MacLean lived. (See Figure 7.6.) She spent a lot of time facilitating learning experiences that combined her passions with the passions of her students. Finding that

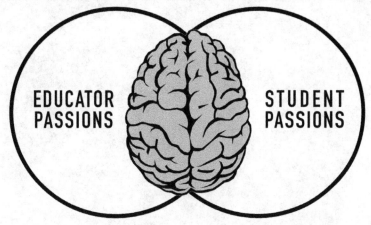

SEEING STRENGTHS AND UNLEASHING THE
PASSIONS OF THE MIND

EDUCATOR
PASSIONS

STUDENT
PASSIONS

[Figure 7.6: Seeing Strengths—Venn Diagram]

common ground with each individual learner requires a relentless pursuit of passion.

Our school is always looking for meaningful ways to take student learning deeper, so we started thinking about combining the passions of students and staff. A couple years ago, a beloved teacher retired from our school after working there for nearly forty years. While she was still teaching, I would occasionally chat with her about her husband's woodworking hobby. Woodworking was his jelly. That's when we decided to tap into his passion to help us amplify our students' passions.

I reached out to the retired teacher's husband, and the concept of a Build-a-Book wall display was born. He constructed a custom LEGO wall containing a book display shelf on the top. Now students

[Figure 7.7: LEGO Book Wall]

can share the books they're reading in a manner that's meaningful to them. (See Figure 7.7.) They're building alternate cover designs and recreating scenes from the books they love.

The Build-a-Book station has been so popular that a high school student created ten portable stations as part of an Eagle Scout project. These portable LEGO walls can be checked out like library books. It's been powerful to hear the conversations kids are having about the books they're reading while they're building together. Last year

Try This!

Think about an element from your work you are passionate about. This could be literacy, coaching, or building relationships with others. Be intentional about seeking out the strengths and passions of others that overlap with your area of interest. Try to envision new ways learning might grow where your passions converge. Collaborate with others to make this a reality.

I was working with a group of boys who had just finished reading *Scar Island* by Dan Gemeinhart. They were using LEGO bricks to recreate the island from the book when a debate erupted about what color bricks to use. They wanted the tone of their project to match the darker plot from the book.

Helping students grow as readers is a task all educators in our building are responsible for. Reading is a foundational skill supporting all subsequent learning. In the Build-a-Book example, by seeing students' jelly, (e.g., building, being social, kinesthetic learning), we were able to reinforce our literacy goals in a manner that was far more effective than any reading log or worksheet packet. As you're putting the Donut Theorem into action, don't get too bogged down by searching out other people's passions; start by finding *your* passion and jelly, and the next steps will fall into place.

Voices from the Field

"I love teaching teachers how to unlock student learning. My goal is to help teachers transform passive-learning environments through active and cooperative learning and purposeful technology integration. I'm passionate about teaching teachers strategies to improve students' behavior, physical health, and mental well-being through movement. Giving up a small amount of instructional time to add brain boosts and movement in the classroom increases learning time."

—Dr. Kristen M. Ford, college professor and department chair of health, PE, and exercise science, Minnesota

I'm not sure if this happens to anyone else, but when I see somebody operating from a place of passion, I tend to pay attention. This is probably why I am consistently inspired by my friend Jennifer LaGarde. I affectionately refer to Jenn as the "Librarian to the Stars" because of the energy and expertise she brings to conversations about reading. Few things get Jenn as excited as chatting about books or the opportunity to design a webpage or avatar. She's a self-professed nerd!

Jenn will be the first to tell you that, like any skill, owning your gifts and thinking about ways you can harness them in your own unique way takes practice. For her, this practice includes actively countering the voices in her head that try to convince her she doesn't have anything worth sharing, or that she'll come off as arrogant if she shares her passions. Jenn tries to look at each new challenge through the lens of what she can uniquely bring to it. This also helps her think about other people whose "jelly" complements her own and whose talents she needs in order to get the work done in the best way possible for kids.

──────PUTTING IT INTO PRACTICE──────

It's important to keep coming back to the learners we serve. There's a difference between being passionate and tapping into your passions to support how others are learning. We must do both.

You might remember the incredible cast Joey managed to bounce off a flagpole while he and I were fishing, but I want to circle back to something we skimmed over. Joey often joked by saying I was out "casting lures" instead of fishing. I want us to apply this same logic to the work we do as educators. We might be teaching and leading, but the people we serve may not be learning and growing. We need to ask ourselves if we are "fishing" or just casting lures!

> ## We need to ask ourselves if we are "fishing" or just casting lures!

When we find our jelly and help those around us find theirs, lasting learning is the result. Over the course of the next month, be intentional about helping others learn and grow. Do this by incorporating your passion and seeking the talents of others regardless of how difficult it might be.

Creating Conversation and Community

If you think back to our opening question at the beginning of this chapter, you can probably understand how students feel when we don't understand or acknowledge their strengths. We also know how positive it feels when others see our strengths.

1. How would Joey's experience have differed if others looked for his strengths before identifying his deficits? How might you train your mind to see the strengths in others so they can more effectively address their weaknesses?
2. How has your school or district deliberately tapped into your jelly? In what ways have you made your jelly known?
3. What are the activities and strategies that help you to tap into the strengths of the learners you serve?

#RECLAIMINGOURCALLING

Resources

1. Narula, Svati Kirsten, "Sushinomics: How Bluefin Tuna Became a Million-Dollar Fish," *The Atlantic,* January 5, 2014, theatlantic.com/international/archive/2014/01/ sushinomics-how-bluefin-tuna-became-a-million-dollar-fish/282826.

2. "Tuna Fishermen Underestimate Risks," *Preaching Today*, preachingtoday.com/illustrations/2005/december/16244.html.

3. "Can you crack the school bus puzzle? This easy brainteaser for kids stumps adults," *Today*, August 29, 2016, today.com/parents/ can-you-crack-school-bus-puzzle-easy-brainteaser-kids-stumps-t71521.

PASSION IV

The Hope
of Education

CHAPTER 8

Hot Dogs and Hope

Backstory

It seems like we could all use a little more *hope* these days. You've probably noticed there are plenty of hope-filled platitudes being tossed around by politicians and educational pundits, but the kind of hope I'm talking about isn't sandwiched between mandates and mudslinging. The hope of education rests in our ability to see school through the eyes of the learners we serve. It's only from a place of deep empathy that meaningful change and innovation can spring.

WHAT IS ONE THING YOU'VE TRIED THAT MIGHT BE CONSIDERED INNOVATIVE TO SOME BUT MAYBE NOT TO OTHERS?

Joey Forrest

When Joey and I were in high school, most of our conversations weren't what you'd consider deep. Every once in a while we'd let our guard down and share something that gave the other person pause. These moments were few and far between, but they definitely had staying power.

When I mentioned Joey had Tourette Syndrome (TS), I alluded to the fact that we all had noticed some of his facial tics in school. This was one reason why some of our teachers needed to have class talks when we were younger. The thing I didn't mention was how Joey himself experienced his tics and everything that accompanied them.

Joey and I were having a sleepover when he shared how hopeless having TS felt at times. The endless twitches, stares from people passing by, and fatigue associated with fighting the involuntary impulses took their toll. As difficult as all of this sounded for my friend, it was what he shared next that really stuck with me.

Joey said he had been reading a popular sports magazine when he came across an article about a famous baseball player. I don't remember who the baseball player was, but I do remember arguing with Joey that the player was *not* famous. Joey vehemently disagreed with me by offering something I couldn't counter: "He's famous to me."

How does one confront that logic?

Joey went on to explain how this "famous" baseball player had TS and still made it to the big leagues. I didn't think this was such a big deal, but it clearly meant something to my friend. Reading about the baseball player helped Joey understand that things could work out okay. He gleaned hope by reading about somebody who was like him.

It's been many years since my friend read that magazine article, but I'll never forget the hope-filled quiver in his voice as he told me about it.

I recently came across a children's novel called *Forget Me Not* by Ellie Terry. It featured a young girl named Calli who also had TS. Almost instantly, that novel took me back in time to that high school sleepover with Joey. In a strange way, it still feels like our conversation happened yesterday.

Reading about Calli reminded me why it is so vital for kids to see themselves in the books they're reading. It turns out hope is not a fleeting feeling, but something real and tangible we can offer our students. I've thought a lot about how this applies to my calling.

When I visit classrooms to do monthly read-alouds, I try to select stories featuring kids with different interests who are from every background, race, and religion. I also try to BookTalk titles that include diverse characters and places our students haven't been before. Hope can be as simple as connecting a child to a book that builds empathy or broadens their horizons.

With this in mind, the simple acts of reading and doing BookTalks for your class will take on a new significance. Sharing the books you love is a lot like recommending an amazing movie to a friend. Share why the book is amazing, but don't give away the ending! BookTalking is such a powerful practice because the books we bless often become the books our students can't wait to read next. Just remember: Students need to see themselves in the books you're sharing with them.

Voices from the Field

"I want to give hope to children who currently do not see the value they hold, especially those who look like me. One way I do this is by sharing my passion for reading so that children can experience worlds unknown."

—LaQuita Outlaw, middle school principal, New York

Try This!

It doesn't matter what age level you work with or the role in which you're serving; try providing students hope in the form of a book they can relate to on a deeper level. Recommending specific titles to individual students is a powerful practice. To do this well, you'll need to read lots of books and connect with others who are doing the same.

When it comes to ensuring students see themselves in their school, books are only the beginning. We need to take a critical look at the artists, composers, and stories students interact with in all content areas. It's such an important shift. When we see school through the eyes of the learner, our ability to make meaningful change a reality is enhanced.

We've All Been There

Sometimes when people talk about making big changes to education, my mind goes to the wrong place. Has this ever happened to you? I cohost a school leadership podcast called *UnearthED* with a friend of mine from Michigan. We had a conversation on the show with Simon T. Bailey that focused on some of the bold things educators are doing for kids.

Here's where I messed up.

Over the course of the entire show, I was thinking "bold things" equated to flashy, high-impact changes. Toward the end of the show, Simon surprised me by sharing a couple innovative ideas that were all substance and *no* flash. It was actually really refreshing; for example, Simon encouraged educators to ask one another what they could do to help instead of beating the drum of change for the sake of change. Simon also suggested sharing student successes with our supervisors and upper administration. It seems so simple, but doing the simple things daily can have a big impact.

Letting Go and Thinking Differently

This past fall we had a family cookout and bonfire in the back-yard. The fire was a little low, so I asked my youngest daughter, Hope, to grab a bundle of firewood from our garage. Admittedly, the pre-packaged bundles of wood we had stored in the garage were probably a little heavier than most other things I might ask her to lift; neverthe-less, she ran up the hill and into the garage.

A few minutes later I heard her rolling the heavy bundle of logs down the hill while proudly proclaiming, "Look, dad; I'm being innovative!"

I'm always surprised by Hope's passion (and loudness), but the unexpected nature of her approach really stuck out in this instance. When we had purchased the bundles of wood, they had come tied together along with a heavy-duty handle stapled into one of the logs. It had never occurred to me a person would transport the wood with-out using the handle.

Later that evening, as we were sitting around the fire, I ran a cou-ple follow-up questions by Hope. I know many educators are noto-rious for these types of conversations, but I couldn't resist. Anyway, here's what I asked Hope:

> Me: What made you think rolling the wood down the
> hill was innovative?
> Hope: (Somewhat accusingly) Are you recording this
> or something?
> Me: (Reassuringly) No. I'm just curious how you know
> if something is innovative.
> Hope: (In a more trusting tone) Something is innovative
> if it's useful, helpful, and unique or different.

In that moment, it appeared as if my daughter had figured out something that still perplexes me. Innovation and flashy new technology are not synonymous. Many of us have reduced innovation to a fraction of its potential by overemphasizing one dimension of it. And students are seeing the same thing done to their schools.

Knowing the Learner

In the first part of this book, I defined the core of our profession in terms of relationships, relevance, identity, and transcendent learning. I actually believe these things represent more than the core of our calling. They represent hope. But even with these core elements (relationships, relevance, identity, and transcendent learning) being identified, it's possible well-intentioned educators will not see eye to eye on the best path forward.

Have you ever experienced this?

It's perfectly natural for passionate people to disagree on what's best for kids. In these moments, it can be tempting to shut your classroom or office door and go about your business. There's no easy answer when two (or more) passionate people disagree, but I offer some cautionary encouragement: The learners you serve, as well as the instructional goals you have for them, are different from the learners and goals I'm working with in my classroom or school. This understanding is vital. It doesn't make either one of us right or wrong; instead, it's an opportunity for a learner-driven dialogue.

When entering into these dialogues, we need to be careful the approach we're advocating for is really about the students in front of us today and not the students we had when we first started teaching. We also need to be sure we're not projecting our own comfort levels, interests, and aspirations on students.

This is something Mrs. MacLean was very careful about. She was keenly aware of her strengths, but even more in tune with her students' passions. One look at her classroom would confirm this; in fact, she was the first person to open my eyes to creating learner-driven environments before that was a thing. She applied so many simple strategies to ensure students could always identify with their space. In a time when many educators were decorating their rooms with the things they were most passionate about (e.g., favorite sport, hobby, animal, or color), Mrs. MacLean made sure her students' passions adorned the walls.

One of my own kids recently took an interest in genetics and DNA. At home, her curiosity is unceasing. She lambasts my wife and me with questions and researches these things during the evening and on weekends.

When she requested books about genetics from school, she didn't get the answer she was hoping for. I don't see this as an indictment against anyone working in her school. It simply points to an opportunity for us to start seeing schools differently. We can't let school be the place where students learn that their passions aren't a priority. The DNA of our schools must include student curiosity and questions. Every process, resource, lesson, and meeting must reflect the learners we are serving.

> ## Try This!
>
> Leave a corner of your classroom or several bulletin boards blank until school starts. Some of the teachers who I get to work with post signs stating, "Under Construction" or "Student Art Coming Soon" to signal to families the work and passions of their children is important.

What if students came to school each day with the expectation that their classrooms and libraries were a work in progress just like they are. What if part of their day was largely represented by their questions and interests? What if learners had more of a say in the books that are purchased or how budgets are built—not as a novelty, but as a consistent practice?

When we commit to trying to see school through students' eyes, we will be nimbler and more inclusive of the learners we serve. One of the most innovative things we can do is reflect upon how our students are experiencing learning. (See Figure 8.1.)

There is a danger in adults being the sole assessors of how real (or innovative) learning is. We really need to get into the habit of looking at things through our students' eyes.

[Figure 8.1: Innovative Educators]

We had a special-education director who unswervingly modeled a learner-driven approach. The topic of the meeting didn't matter; she always mentioned student perspective. She helped us consider how students with special needs might experience things as a result of any action (or inaction) on our part. It didn't matter if we were planning professional development or discussing math intervention; her consistent commitment to entering the conversation with a student lens in mind was one of the most innovative things I've encountered in education.

It actually got to the point where we would speak for her when she was not at a meeting by speculating, "If [she] were here, we would need to think about this from the perspective of a student with special needs." The best part of her legacy is how her work and thinking lives on because she built this capacity into us all. I'm not suggesting this type of meaningful change was easy; no daily discipline is. I am, however, encouraged by the fact that one person can create meaningful change through empathy and a learner-driven lens.

Before we go too much further, I want to be sure to frame innovation as the hope-inducing thing it can be. Here's the definition for innovation I like to use:

Innovation is the process and thinking that makes meaningful change possible. It is an opportunity to see school through the eyes of the learner and the responsibility to do things differently as a result. It is rarely a *thing*.

> *Innovation is the process and thinking that makes meaningful change possible. It is an opportunity to see school through the eyes of the learner and the responsibility to do things differently as a result. It is rarely a thing.*

An inseparable link bonds innovation and meaningful change. This link is where hope resides. Those who have experienced meaningful change understand that it is far more than a buzzword.

Did You Know?

We're about to embark on the best data-driven dialogue you've ever experienced, but allow me to share the backstory first. Each year our school revises our master schedule based on staffing changes, enrollment, and the classes we plan to offer. I was reviewing last year's schedule and wanting to make some improvements. I occasionally get feedback from families indicating some of our youngest learners need a little more time to eat their lunch. (The dad in me totally gets this because I've seen my own kids take two hours to eat half a sandwich.)

After receiving this feedback, I was intent on finding a way to get students more time to eat in our cafeteria. To tackle this problem, I did what any accomplished educator would do. I Googled it. It didn't take long for my Google search to get off track.

That's when I stumbled upon the best-kept secret on the Internet.

Each year an elite field of competitive eaters converges on New York City for Nathan's Hot Dog Eating Contest. The contest pits twenty people against one another with one goal; to see who can eat the most hot dogs and buns in ten minutes. My research also revealed contest organizers previously gave competitors twelve minutes to scarf down as many dogs as possible, but have since reduced the time to just ten minutes. Over the past several decades, the winner has consumed anywhere between fifteen and seventy-four hot dogs! This got me thinking, *If one person can eat seventy-four hot dogs in ten minutes, our students should be able to eat five mini-corn dogs in twenty minutes. Right?!*

Here's where we bring in that data-driven dialogue I promised. For the past twenty years or so, the contest has been dominated by two contestants; Takeru Kobayashi and Joey "Jaws" Chestnut. Joey is the world champion who downed seventy-four hot dogs and buns in ten minutes in 2018. In the late 1990s, the world record was around twenty-five, but in the early 2000s that record was nearly doubled. (See Figure 8.2.) That's because innovation was applied to the process.[1]

When I defined innovation as the process and thinking that makes meaningful change possible, I did so intentionally to emphasize the importance of the people and process involved in change. That's because *the people and process* are often *the progress.*

You might be wondering what changed in the hot dog eating process that led to such dramatically different results? The contestant who goes by the name "Kobayashi" introduced advanced

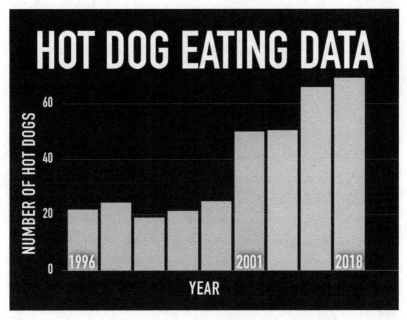

[Figure 8.2: Hot Dog Eating Data]

Voices from the Field

"The main thing I've let go of are limits for myself and students. I've witnessed the limitless potential students have, and it's driven me to create more open-ended assignments, so now when I tell students to do their best, they actually have the opportunity to do their best."

—Martin Son,
middle school math
teacher, Illinois

eating techniques to the event. Joey Chestnut improved upon Kobayashi's training techniques, and the two have transformed the training process most competitive eaters use now.

In case you're wanting to expand your eating abilities, here's how the pros do it: After consulting with their doctors, competitors prepare months in advance by downing gallons of milk to increase stomach capacity and train their bodies to fight the gag reflex. They break hot dogs in half and simultaneously stuff both halves side-by-side in their mouths to increase efficiency. Hot dog buns are dipped in water and consumed separately.[2] All of these innovations lead to greater achievement gains (a.k.a. hot dog consumption increases).

Onward and Upward

The innovation involved in hot dog eating is definitely process oriented. This doesn't mean tools themselves can't lead to meaningful change. As a quick aside, Olympic Pole Vaulters were previously averaging around ten feet of clearance using wooden poles. With each technological breakthrough, those heights increased. (See Figure 8.3.)

It appears that every forty to fifty years, the introduction of a new pole-vaulting technology led to a breakthrough in achievement. All of this has me wondering a few things: What's next after fiberglass, and

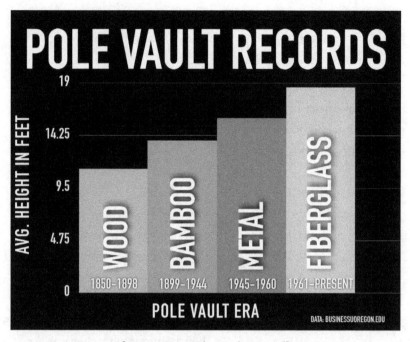

[Figure 8.3: Pole Vault Record]

will we see anyone pole vault close to thirty feet in our lifetime? More importantly, are we still teaching and leading with "metal" methodology when fiberglass is available? If so, we are limiting our students.

We can create the conditions where students are leading innovation and meaningful change, but it starts with how we're leading (or possibly limiting) ourselves. It's important to note that your approach to this work will be different from how others approach it. Meaningful change is always context specific.

I'm going to share four levers to meaningful change that can be adapted to a variety of contexts. Each lever is accompanied by an example that may (or may not) be innovative compared to the work you and your team are doing. Instead of reading the examples to evaluate how innovative (or "uninnovative") they are, I'm going to ask you to think about the following:

- Are the levers themselves process oriented, product oriented, or learner driven?
- How might students view the changes described in each of the four examples?

Lever #1: Practice a Pedagogy of Choice

You can almost feel when it's Friday in a school. When I was teaching, part of our grade-level team changed how we planned for Friday afternoons. We started planning unique learning experiences appealing to the strengths students had. Students from several classes signed up to attend sessions they were interested in regardless of who their homeroom teacher was.

We referred to this Friday choice time as "KidSmart" because the sessions were based on Howard Gardner's Multiple Intelligence Theory. We believed every learner came to us with innate intelligence our grade-level assessments didn't always detect. KidSmart was our way of creating the conditions for students to see their strengths and make choices that mattered to them.

Try This!

Giving students more choice doesn't need to involve an extravagant array of enrichment classes or options. If you have a designated "take a break" space in your classroom, try providing students a choice in where to take their breaks. If you plan to show a movie every once in a while, try partnering with a colleague so your students can choose from a couple different options.

Lever #2: Repurpose Existing Resources

Repurposing existing resources led to one of the most meaningful changes I ever made as a teacher. I asked my principal at the time if I could purchase hands-on math manipulatives (e.g., games, creative construction materials, and supplies) instead of consumable workbooks. She agreed, and from that year on, we dedicated the money that would have gone into consumable math workbooks to materials that elicited more learner engagement.

Over the course of six years or so, I created standards-based learning experiences that helped students learn mathematics at a deeper level than any workbook page ever had. There were times we used notebooks, graph paper, and mini-whiteboards for practice, but the bulk of the budget paid for a myriad of ways students could interact with key concepts and one another. In a subject that can feel hopeless for some students, our math class became a space where the budget supported the core of our calling.

> ## Try This!
>
> Consistently being told to do more with less can be demoralizing. Reframe that idea by looking for opportunities to *do differently* with the same. Think about existing resources (e.g., time, budget, talents, and supplies), then collaborate with a colleague on any meaningful changes you might like to try.

Lever #3: Prioritize Content Creation

One way our school has leveraged content creation is through a fleet of mobile MakerSpace carts that can be checked out like library books. The carts contain resources like LEGO bricks, knitting looms, 3-D printers, Play-Doh, robotic droids, drones, K'NEX, cardboard, PVC pipe, and books related to each resource. I wrote extensively about how we're using the carts in my book *Renegade Leadership*, but for those of you who may not be familiar with that book, the idea behind the carts is simple. Our team wanted to provide students the opportunity to collaborate and create in every classroom and hallway in our school. We started with four carts and now have around eighteen to twenty.

In the past couple years, we also added a "Digital-Content Creation" cart to our fleet. The resources on the carts work in concert with students' inclination to communicate, create, and share:

- Students are creating videos in social studies class using a greenscreen to show what they're learning about natural disasters. Their interest in the production process has fueled deeper learning.
- Countless students are creating engaging videos featuring the books they're reading. Their BookTalk videos help classmates connect to books they might find interesting and develop communication skills and learning that lasts.
- One student created a mathematical video tutorial demonstrating how to calculate the perimeter of a playground using a drone. The entire experience was made possible by a teacher committed to finding each student's jelly.
- A class narrated the journey of a food particle (represented by a robotic droid) as it traveled through different parts of the digestive system. Students created a video of the robotic droid as it navigated a giant floor mural depicting the digestive system they had created in health class.
- A group of students created a virtual reality (VR) quest that took viewers on an immersive journey through the Media Center. The quest was an extension of work they had done in language arts and also part of our school's BookCast video series.

The carts have helped us support a culture of creativity and innovation by increasing the opportunities for this type of learning. They've also given us additional means to help students learn through inventing, engineering, and failure, but it has never really been about the carts.

One of the questions our team hears most from visiting educators relates to the perception their colleagues have about hands-on learning. Visiting educators wonder whether their principals see the same value in *making* as they do in more traditional paper-pencil work. I created a Taxonomy of Making to help educators talk about the value in all the levels of content creation. (See Figure 8.4.)

Just because a student might be driving part of the process does not invalidate the learning (or teaching). The same holds true for teacher-directed learning. The more we practice using the lever of content creation, the more proficient we'll become in facilitating and sharing it.

—*Try This!*

Take one lesson or staff meeting and inject additional opportunities for participants to learn through making. Content creation can involve digital designs, audio, video, or more tactile projects. The key is to support learning through active, hands-on processes. (Don't forget to share your maker transformation with us on our community hashtag.)

Lever #4: Amplify Student Voice

Student voice, in my opinion, is one of the strongest drivers of learning that lasts. When we empower students to communicate their ideas with an audience that's authentic to them, we provide them the hope that they can dream and do anything. This final example is more of a pinnacle-type story that was only made possible by years of

[Figure 8.4: Taxonomy of Making]

important work done by our staff, but it highlights the kinds of experiences for which we prepare students when our system and processes are learner driven.

I was attending one of Minnesota's largest gatherings for principals, and although I didn't have the best seat, there was no mistaking the red toy airplane sitting ominously on stage. That's because I knew the airplane belonged to one of our former students, Ethan, who happened to be in middle school at the time of the conference.

As Ethan took the stage, memories flooded my mind. I thought back to the times I'd pass by him in the hallway as he was learning to read, write, and share his ideas with the world. I reflected on some of the video production projects he and I had worked on in my office over the years. But most of all, I remembered all the teachers who invested in him along the way. In my mind, this was their stage as much as it was his.

I desperately wanted his presentation to go well. I knew how hard he had prepared. I also knew he was uniquely equipped to deliver his message, which he had titled "Achievement that Lasts." Not surprisingly, his ten-minute talk turned out to be one of the most memorable from the entire conference.

He absolutely crushed it!

It's one thing for the adults in a school to talk about student empowerment, but it is an entirely different thing for a student to educate school leaders on the importance of learning that lasts. When I think back to seeing a former student on stage sharing his message with several hundred principals, my mind inevitably recalls all the ways our team amplified his voice from an early age.[3]

Try This!

Identify one routine or tradition in your classroom or school that students could take more ownership of. The possibilities are endless! You could try inviting students to help lead tours, participate in PD, manage morning meetings, take over your technology help desk, share speeches, kick off staff meetings, sing the anthem prior to events, or lead school assemblies . . . the energy and insights students bring to this conversation will change the very culture of your classroom or school.

Liz

The four levers above demonstrate how meaningful change is possible when we tap into pedagogy, resources, content creation, and student voice. Unfortunately, most of us can attest to what happens when we start pulling levers simply for the sake of change.

By now I've probably made it sound like Liz's official volunteer job description included walking on water. That's how highly I thought of her. It's safe to say we had our share of disagreements too. Liz and I each loved to cook, so this was a topic we discussed often. One day Liz shared something she had heard on a popular daytime cooking show. Evidently, a person can substitute pumpkin filling for eggs in chocolate-cake recipes. She must have sensed my skepticism because she proceeded to tell me all the health benefits and cited how the TV host had said the difference was indiscernible. I ended up stopping at the grocery store on the drive home to pick up some chocolate frosting, cake mix, and pumpkin filling—but no eggs.

After my eggless cake cooled, I frosted it and placed a couple scoops of vanilla bean ice-cream on a plate. I was excited to sink my teeth into the cake and compare notes with Liz the next time she volunteered in our class.

Until I took my first bite.

The recipe was a complete bust, and the change from eggs to canned pumpkin was a very bad idea. This was one innovation the world could do without. Liz's son has since graduated high school, but each time our paths cross, I try to reference pumpkin filling in some capacity.

The reason I share this story is to emphasize how some ingredients and practices will always be important in schools. Obviously, there are some things students are counting on us to re-evaluate, but we would do well *not* to change things for the sake of change.

More Than a Number

Most educators do not have a problem with assessments that are meaningful. The problem of practice we all must reconcile is testing that competes with our goals for student success.

For years, business leaders have talked about a powerful way to accomplish seemingly competing goals. I've heard educators adopt this approach as well. With one small word, we can tap into the immense value in meaningful assessment practices while acknowledging we have a long way to go in meeting the needs of the whole learner. The small word everyone seems to be talking about is *and*.

Here's how I see the power of *and* enhancing our thinking around assessment:

- We need to help students learn at a high level *and* become persons of high character.
- We want students engaged in their learning *and* empowered to make a difference in their world.
- We will teach for content mastery *and* tap into new processes, innovative thinking, and responsible risk-taking.

PUTTING IT INTO PRACTICE

The hope of education can be found in our ability to pair long-standing priorities with new possibilities. The levers for meaningful change are within reach when we see school through the eyes of the learner.

Try to apply innovation to best practice using the power of *and*. Consider pairing one (or more) of the levers we looked at with one element of the learning experience. You might find a way to further amplify student voice in a lesson or staff meeting or make a commitment to embedding content creation into your work on a more consistent basis. Whatever you decide to do, I'd love to hear how things progress for you and your students.

Creating Conversation and Community

The hope of education rests in our commitment to see school through the eyes of the learner. This might be the single-most innovative and meaningful thing we can do.

1. I gave Liz a hard time for changing a recipe for the sake of change. What are some examples of "innovation" that have been meaningful for you?

2. How are hope and innovation the same? How are they different?

3. When you think about how the learners you serve are experiencing their space, materials, and school routines, what is one thing they might hope to see changed? (Don't forget to ask them!)

#ReclaimingOurCalling

Resources

1. "Hall of Fame," *Nathan's,* accessed Sept. 24, 2018, nathansfamous.com/promos-and-fanfare/hot-dog-eating-contest/hall-of-fame.

2. "Nathan's Hot Dog Eating Contest," *Wikipedia,* accessed Sept. 24, 2018, en.wikipedia.org/wiki/Nathan%27s_Hot_Dog_Eating_Contest.

3. Gustafson, Brad, "The Best Part of Our Story Is You," *Adjusting Course,* April 11, 2018, bradgustafson.com/single-post/2018/04/11/The-Best-Part-of-Our-Story-is-You.

Loose Ends and Legacy

Backstory

At this point, I'd like to tie up some loose ends and highlight a few of the things I *hope* you'll remember most. First, our legacy is defined by what we empower others to do. Our impact is not always noticed immediately, and sometimes it spans multiple generations without us being aware. Our students are counting on us to reclaim our calling, so each of the loose ends that follows is accompanied by questions to inspire hope, elicit reflection, and empower others.

Analogous to Teaching

If a caterpillar falls into standing water, it can easily drown. But it's possible to revive a caterpillar if it has not been underwater too long. By gently drying the caterpillar's body and then covering it with salt, a person can draw the excess water out of the tiny animal's spiracles and trachea. This allows air to enter again, essentially breathing new life into the tiny animal.[1]

Whom (or what) do you think the caterpillar represents in the analogy above? I suppose it could be our students, their schools, or maybe even you and me. Hope never dies, and our calling can always be revived. If we don't work on behalf of the whole learner, some students will flounder through school—or potentially drown in a school system that doesn't see them. But there is hope, and we can help these students breathe again.

If you listen carefully, you'll hear signs that some of our colleagues are drowning too. Our comrades are caving against the torrent of student needs, increasing accountability, and ever-growing to-do lists. The heaviness of the world our students inhabit isn't helping either. Our empathy and resolve remain high, but burnout becomes a reality when we're expected to work harder at the things that don't seem to help our students.

It's simply not possible to split our allegiances. There's a prophetic verse in the Bible that warns, "No one can serve two masters; for either he will hate the one and love the other, or else he will be loyal to the one and despise the other (Matthew 6:24)." We need to serve on behalf of the whole learner. The learner is first; everything else comes next. This is what learning that lasts is all about.

Questions to Inspire Hope and Elicit Reflection

- What would happen if we approached the broken areas of our work and lives like the caterpillar described above?

- When is the last time you had an honest conversation with your colleagues or supervisor about hope and the areas in which you need help?

Mrs. MacLean's Last Stand

Books and riddles aside, the most magnetic thing about Mrs. MacLean was how she brought people together. But coming together was only the starting point; her goal was always to create something that mattered.

Mrs. MacLean seemed to know something about school many experts haven't figured out yet. When she spoke about her students (and her own PD), she'd often say, "People don't like when decisions are made for them or about them, without them."

People appreciate being included in decisions impacting their life's work. Mrs. MacLean knew she liked to be involved in decisions, so she extended the same courtesy to her class. This simple act seemed to strengthen the relationships she had with students. At the same time, it made their learning more relevant because they were an integral part of creating those experiences. What distinguished her from other educators was how she lived out the idea that relationships are the foundation of anything worthwhile, but they are not the end goal. It was always about building something better together.

I'm confident we all share some of the same beliefs and idiosyncrasies that made Mrs. MacLean so effective. Mrs. MacLean valued people and always tried to speak the truth in a loving manner (which is a lot different from just being right). She was an ambassador of trust, and her approach made transcendent learning possible. The truth is, she has a little bit of all of us in her.

Questions to Inspire Hope and Elicit Reflection

- Is there anyone you need to get to know better before trying to teach or lead them?
- How do you include others in decisions about their work and learning?
- Would your students say you extend them the same respect and input you expect from others?

A Final Ode to Kenny Mauer

Education is the beginning and end of all we aspire for our students. Our classrooms contain countless numbers of kids waiting for you and me to help make school meaningful to each and every one of them. They're waiting for us to protect them, to help them better understand themselves, and increase their capacity to appreciate the multitude of different backgrounds and belief systems in the world.

When we were in school, Kenny Mauer and I never really hit it off. And it wasn't (just) because he turned my Show and Tell moment into "Underwear Gate" either. It was because I despised the way he diminished Joey.

Not surprisingly, Kenny's interest in music, fashion, and after-school activities became increasingly different from ours. He stuck with the Goth look and heavy metal while Joey and I spent our mornings pinning the bottoms of our stonewashed blue jeans. (If you are not a child of the '80s, that last part will not make any sense.)

Although it's been more than twenty years since we graduated high school, I've only had the *pleasure* of running into Kenny twice. Shortly after college, we were at the same bachelor party. The party was an epic, two-day fishing tournament arranged by a mutual friend. (You can't choose your friend's friends, right?) Everyone kicked in some money, and we agreed in advance the groom would take home half of the grand prize. The winning team would split the rest.

Five or six boats were involved, and as luck would have it, Joey and I were put in the same boat as Kenny. The idea was that every team would have a member of an opposing team fishing in their boat to ensure adherence to tournament rules. (The irony of Kenny Mauer "policing" anything is still not lost on me.)

I'll never forget this next part: Joey was operating his trolling motor using a foot pedal while Kenny and I were arguing about something related to the tournament. Kenny had a couple beers in him and was being even more belligerent than usual. As Kenny heaved his line toward a partially submerged tree, the boat subtly shifted. I caught my balance in time to see a small smirk appear on Joey's face—just as Kenny toppled into the lake.

This is horrible of me to admit, but I will always cherish the memory of seeing Kenny's freckled face gasping for air as he frantically tried to find his way to the side of Joey's boat. It may not have been obvious to Kenny, but my friend knew his boat like nobody else. If Joey wanted to eject a passenger without the person knowing it, he could. And he did. As Joey and I stared at our nemesis in the water, it was clear he had lost his power over us.

The tides had definitely turned for Joey.

My second run-in with Kenny came years later. My wife and I had flown to a concert in Texas to meet up with some friends. Evidently Kenny's taste in music had improved since high school, because I saw him in line ahead of us at the concert. I had heard rumors he had moved to the Lone Star State, but I didn't go out of my way to talk to him.

Best to let sleeping dogs lie, I guess.

While we were waiting in line, I couldn't help but notice the number of concert goers wearing cowboy boots. Since many of them appeared older than I (and slightly less flexible), I started thinking about that issue I mentioned earlier. Remember those boots I got for my fortieth birthday in Nashville? I still have a hard time prying them off, so I was wondering how in the world people who appeared a little less agile got their boots off? Seriously. After asking around, it turns out there is a tool called a "boot wedge" that helps a person's boots glide off like butter.

Who knew?

This wasn't the only thing I learned at that concert. Seeing Kenny Mauer again made me reflect on all the different people at that concert. I've heard it said that nothing brings people together like music and sports. I suppose, to a certain extent, this is true. But not even the Super Bowl brings people together like education.

It's an incredible calling. Not only do our students come together to learn, but they occupy the same spaces (physical and virtual) as people with drastically different ideas and belief systems. When you think about it, education is the most important shared experience there is, and we're helping to lead it.

Questions to Inspire Hope and Elicit Reflection

- How do you teach students to learn?
- What would happen if the act of coming together to *do* school was so powerful, students didn't want it to stop?
- How else could you make school more meaningful to the students you serve?

All Still Means ALL

The world moves too fast at times. As daunting as the changes in education might feel, it's important to think about all the things educators do that will always be important.

Gary Speese grew up in an urban neighborhood in Kansas City, Missouri. He had three main places he loved to be: school, church, and the Boy's Club community center. The thing Gary remembers most about these places is the loving adults who always acknowledged young people.

At school, the teachers, counselors, coaches, and security guards would greet him and inquire about his classes and family. During these brief exchanges, they always seemed to expect Gary to go into enough detail to make the conversation meaningful. This only took thirty to sixty seconds, but Gary recalls them being formative to his development. They saw attributes in Gary (like honesty, integrity, curiosity, and kindness) before he saw them in himself. Several adults who greeted Gary in this manner made it very clear to him that he mattered. They would say, "Gary, you are going to be somebody one day." And they were right.

Gary is now an educator. He's currently serving as an assistant high school principal in Minnesota. I had the chance to sit down and visit with him recently and was inspired by his journey. He also made it clear things weren't always sunshine and roses.

There were times, Gary recalled, when he ran his mouth or got into fights. The same educators who took time to tell him he mattered also took time to discipline him. Sometimes this involved a short conversation and a one-minute reprimand, and other times it involved a paddle. They always stood by Gary and expected him to reflect on his behavior. When he'd see them again, they checked in on what he had learned and continued to confirm his positive character traits.

It was clear Gary cherished his experience growing up in an urban community. The thing he kept coming back to in our conversations was the people. What might have seemed like a quick conversation to some of Gary's teachers meant the world to him.

Questions to Inspire Hope and Elicit Reflection

- Given what you know about Gary's story, how might you look at your to-do list differently?
- Are you giving yourself credit for the countless conversations you have had with students already?
- How would you explain the way you connect with students to a newer teacher who was interested in doing the same?

About That Tattoo

Education cannot be in the business of sucking the joy out of learning and replacing it with a label or number. We are culpable when we reduce what we do to data, but only if we allow data to be the end of the story.

Kids are not numbers, and neither are you. You are a work in progress who cannot be defined by one choice, one number, or somebody else's definition of "proficient." This sentiment needs to be put in ink and worn like a badge of courage. Lasting learning and vision attainment require bold beliefs. These are things *not* born from the status quo.

Bold beliefs are worth repeating, and positive redundancy can have the effect of awakening things inside us we already know, so this is my reminder and encouragement to you:

WHAT WOULD SCHOOL LOOK LIKE IF WE HELD THE WHOLE LEARNER

IN THE SAME REGARD AS HIGH-STAKES TEST SCORES?

We would do well to live out our beliefs in a visible and consistent manner. If it's a change worth leading, don't write it in pencil and tuck it in your desk drawer. Put it in ink and allow it to inform every decision you make.

Questions to Inspire Hope and Elicit Reflection

- I've heard people with tattoos quip, "I'll show you mine if you show me yours." In the same spirit of sharing, what's your tattoo or mantra?

Another "Twern"

There are a few things we should never underestimate. Humor is one of those things. In light of that truth, I have a story for you.

I was attending the National Principals Conference in Philadelphia and decided to rent an Airbnb with another principal and his wife who are good friends of ours. It just so happened their flight was delayed, so my wife and I had time to try a practical joke we had talked about prior to the trip.

Since my wife and I arrived at the Airbnb first, we claimed our room by unloading our luggage and hanging a few things up. We then pulled out a special prop and proceeded to walk upstairs to the bedroom our friends would be occupying. We carefully pulled back the comforter on their bed and placed a red, white, and blue Speedo where they'd be sleeping. Before you get any crazy ideas, the Speedo was a gag gift I had received fifteen years earlier when my wife and I were first married. (Our honeymoon was in the Dominican Republic, and my relatives joked that the red, white, and blue swimsuit would be the perfect touch for the trip.)

After carefully positioning the Speedo under our friends' comforter, we remade their bed and giddily walked back downstairs, unable to contain ourselves. When our friends arrived later that night, we went out to dinner and came back to the Airbnb to chat some more before eventually hitting the hay.

As our friends headed upstairs, my wife and I managed to mask our laughter long enough to avoid suspicion. It was late, but we waited for our friends to acknowledge our masterful prank or offer some form of retaliation. Seconds turned to minutes, and all we heard in between our suppressed giggles was silence from upstairs.

We resigned to the fact that our friends might not have discovered the Speedo in their sheets, but we continued taking turns spontaneously erupting in laughter every few minutes for the next hour or so before we both fell asleep.

The following morning, my wife and I discovered the real reason we hadn't heard from our friends. They had discovered "it" right away, but instead of suspecting us, they somehow thought the Airbnb had not been cleaned or laundered properly from the previous occupants' stay. We learned they didn't get much sleep and even had a heated exchange about the possibility of getting a different Airbnb that night.

We all had a good laugh once we clarified our role in the prank. This memory still makes me smile, but I wanted to focus on a subtlety you might not have noticed. I started out this "twern" by stating there are a few things we should never underestimate, and I want to circle back to that. Although it was incredibly childish and very silly, my wife and I committed to executing this prank prior to knowing exactly how we'd be able to pull it off. We didn't know our friends' plane would be delayed, but we also never expected to experience such joy as a result of the laugh we all had together.

There is a parallel here.

Too often in education, we plan things to death, and good ideas stall out because stakeholders can't agree on all the details. Sometimes we just need to decide on something and take a leap of faith forward without having a proactive solution to every foreseeable challenge.

Questions to Inspire Hope and Elicit Reflection

- What's one idea or dream on which your students need you to move forward even if you don't have all the details perfectly planned?

- What brings you joy?
- How have you helped your students and colleagues smile?

Remembering Liz

I've had the chance to receive some colorful emails and be part of some difficult conversations with parents over the course of my teaching, coaching, and administrative career. Many of these meetings involved requests from parents with whom I didn't agree or couldn't honor. But I can't remember a single time when any parent ever asked (or demanded) something for any reason other than the fact that they loved their child.

I mentioned something Liz once quipped earlier in the book, but it feels like a loose end needing further explanation. When Liz said, "You'll see things differently when you have kids of your own, Brad." I didn't grasp what she meant back then, but I think I might have an idea now. Parents are able to see their children in a different light than educators. (I understand this works both ways, but I need more practice seeing things from their perspective, not mine.)

The experience and perspective that parents possess puts them in a unique position to see things in the way their child is experiencing them. This insight lends itself to a level of empathy that is not bound by classroom rules, school budgets, and district policy. A parent's love is one of the purest forms of hope found in a school.

Over the years, I've learned this in the most humbling ways.

I used to be the first person in parent meetings to counter concerns parents were sharing with what we were seeing in school; for example, when a parent would desperately describe the tears, meltdowns, or anxiety they were seeing at home, I'd earnestly offer, "We see your child smiling throughout the school day."

It wasn't until I had the opportunity to see one of my own children battling her challenges at home that I realized how irrelevant it was for me to dismiss any parent's experience. We need to listen to parents when they share how their children are seeing and experiencing school and consider their perspectives—even if we have a different perspective. (This is coming from a principal who also tries to fervently support his staff during difficult parent meetings as well.)

Parents are vital partners in enhancing our vision, perspective, and ability to see school differently. They can help move us one step closer to seeing school through the eyes of the learners we serve.

Questions to Inspire Hope and Elicit Reflection

- If we look at [insert any issue here] from the perspective of a parent, what would they want us to see and understand?
- How might I put this new insight to work to better meet the needs of this learner?
- When I enter difficult parent meetings, am I subconsciously trying to win or seeking to understand?

Back to Taekwondo

Hyper-focusing on a limited view of student learning is one of the worst things we can do as educators. Learning that lasts requires us to look at students' abilities and needs in light of what they need to be successful today, tomorrow, and long after testing season.

I shared one of my proudest moments as a parent in the first part of this book. My daughter had just received a special nomination for a Junior Leadership Award at our state's annual taekwondo banquet. The nomination meant a great deal to my wife and me because it provided hope that she could experience success in life.

I told you they called her name over the loudspeaker in that gigantic banquet hall, but I haven't shared what happened after the awards ceremony yet. A few fellow nominees approached our daughter and requested a picture with her. Already overcome with emotion, I quietly observed how our daughter responded to their request: She graciously agreed, and simultaneously slid her trophy out of the picture and picked up her nomination certificate.

The girls who were in the picture were holding similar nomination certificates. The act of sliding aside her trophy was our daughter's way of showing deference and empathy for the girls.

For my wife and me, this moment of humility was bigger than actually winning the Junior Leadership Award. It was a sign some of the other social skills we were trying desperately to cultivate were in there somewhere. In a moment when it mattered most, our daughter tapped into some of the skills that do not always come easily to her. Seeing this interaction caused me to cry tears on top of tears.

Soft skills like empathy, leadership, and teamwork may not be part of the next round of high-stakes testing, but my guess is your hopes and dreams for students go beyond filling in bubbles. Every great teacher understands that education is so much more than academic knowledge alone.

Questions to Inspire Hope and Elicit Reflection

- How will you teach, lead, and learn on behalf of the whole learner?
- What have you found most effective in teaching all students to learn at a high level while also cultivating positive character?

For Joey

As a hiring administrator, I have the opportunity to interview more than one hundred applicants each school year. If there's one thing I've found, it's the difference between a candidate who knows their strengths and somebody who hasn't found their jelly yet. The difference between candidates who are committed to finding their students' strengths and those who don't consistently think about students' strengths is even more pronounced.

If there's one person whose jelly I know better than anyone else's, it is Joey Forrest. I've told you quite a bit about my friend, but it's been difficult to decide what stories to share; in fact, writing this book about him has been one of the hardest things I've ever done.

That's because I am the one who has the neurological disorder called Tourette Syndrome (TS). It was my elementary teachers who needed to have "the talk" with my classmates so they wouldn't stare at me when my face twitched or my neck cranked in school. And it was me who rattled off a staggering number of sit-ups in PE class while my teacher took one for the team by holding my feet.

Things have gotten progressively better over the years, but I'll never forget the things that gave me hope when I was a child. My mom was always so gracious. She would reassure me things would be okay and helped me find calming activities when my tics would take over. There was also that magazine article featuring the baseball player who had TS. Seeing somebody like me succeed in anything other than sticking out filled me with hope.

And there was one other thing that gave me hope: It was every teacher I ever had who knew me, found my jelly, and let me share it with the world. My teachers were an incredible influence who collectively helped me to see who I was, and more importantly, who I wasn't.

Questions to Inspire Hope and Elicit Reflection

- How might we help students see themselves in every aspect of school (i.e. from the artists, authors, and historic figures they study to the tools and processes they choose to learn with)?

- Given what you know about "jelly," what will you do differently tomorrow to provide hope to the students you serve?

Legacy

Before our time together comes to a close, I wanted to address the elephant in education. Many of the messages we see in the media are being spewed from individuals who haven't stepped foot in a classroom since they were students. And most importantly, they haven't stepped foot in *your* classroom or school. It's not that their opinions don't count. They do.

But we cannot allow them to determine our legacy.

Our legacy must be forged from the things that make up transcendent learning. While the commentary about what *should* be happening in our classrooms continues, let us not lose sight of who is most qualified to make decisions impacting students. The voices from afar cannot be consistently elevated above and beyond the people doing the work.

In all you do, let your light shine and always remember it takes a combination of heart, mind, and hope to facilitate learning that lasts. Hold on to these things with all your might, and encourage those new to this profession to do the same. May your legacy be forged from your ability to respond to your calling in the most complete and learner-driven manner possible.

On Behalf of the Whole Learner,

Resources

1. "Reviving a Drowned Caterpillar," *Butterfly Fun Facts,* butterfly-fun-facts. com/raising-butterflies/tips-to-raising-butterfly-caterpillars-indoors/ reviving-a-drowned-caterpillar.

Thank You

My appreciation

Somebody once said we are a combination of the five people we spend the most time with. This book is a reflection of some of the people I've been blessed to work with the past few years. But first, I want to thank some of the children's book authors who have inspired me. Thanks to Alan Gratz for helping me to think differently about writing and storytelling. Thank you to Ellie Terry and Dusti Bowling for writing hope-filled novels featuring children with TS. Thank you to Phil Bildner and Dav Pilkey for being more than fantastic authors; your mentoring helped make the foreword to this book possible for Paolo.

My fellow disruptors and connectors

I want to thank Chris Dodge for helping me rethink book studies. His innovative thinking led to the launch of the Underground Book Club. I won't deluge you with details here, but suffice it to say, Chris created the type of book study I've always wanted to be part of. Thank you to Danny "Sunshine" Bauer for collaborating on a podcast series to support readers interested in taking their learning deeper. Your willingness to serve and support the creation of compelling audio content for our *Build Your Own Book Study*, is appreciated.

My comrades and contributors

I want to thank all of the educators who contributed to this book. Reading your submissions, hearing your heart, and getting a glimpse into your thinking was nothing short of inspiring. Your voices contributed important perspective and pushed me to think differently about my own practices.

My publisher

Special thanks to the IMPress publishing team for your unswerving support. I knew the book I wanted to write was *different*. Honestly, I worried it was too different. Too storied. Too artistic and personal. I also knew I needed a special team to help me make sense of the best parts of all this "different." Paige and George Couros and Erin Casey did all that and more.

My Dave Burgess Consulting, Inc. people

Through it all, the DBC team was in the background supporting the process. Thanks to our Pirate Leader, Shelley Burgess, for the encouragement and consultation at key decision-points. Parts of this book seemed so unconventional we needed another perspective to ensure we weren't crazy. (The jury is still out on that, but at least the book is in print.)

My friend

I'm a better version of myself thanks to my friend, Jennifer LaGarde. She is one of the most talented and unassuming people I know. I imagine God chuckled when He brought our professional lives together. Jenn is an immense source of good and positive force for literacy in a world that desperately needs it. The fact she tolerates me as a co-collaborator on so many projects still amazes me!

My literacy role models

Seeing teachers change the lives of their students is awe-inspiring, but having my own life changed is something that makes saying "thank you" seem inadequate. Heartfelt thanks to Julie Kirchner and Linda Gibbons for being my own personal *book whisperers* and living out their passion for literacy in such a visible manner. They modeled the way and, to the best of my ability, I followed their lead.

My school family

I could not ask for a more passionate school or team to serve alongside. You've shown me what it means to live for something bigger, to dream bolder, and to keep the whole learner at the center of every conversation. The questions you ask me (and one another) have been a catalyst for truly transformative learning.

My children

Elise, Hope, and Finn – you are my world. Each of you has been uniquely created, and it's been a pure joy to see you start to share your gifts with the world. Thank you for allowing me to share some of your art and stories in this book as well. I could not be more proud to be your dad.

My wife

Lastly, this book would not be possible without the steadfast support and sacrificial giving of my wife, Deb. Her job titles are many and her faith is deep. She is an uncanny judge of character and sometimes knows me better than I know myself. She has encouraged me to embrace how I've been hard-wired and stick to the mission-driven work I feel called to do on behalf of all kids. Thank you, Deb!

Notes

MY JELLY LIST

Hidden Track

Backstory

When I was in college, I remember discovering a hidden track at the end of one of my Pearl Jam CDs. I felt pretty darn cool when I stumbled upon the bonus content. I thought I'd return the favor with an interactive story and a few bonus "tterns."

What Would You Do?

One winter morning in Minnesota, I pulled into a prime parking space—a sign that the in-service training I was attending that day was going to be great. I grabbed my mug of water, tablet, and car keys, and opened my car door. Before I got out, I remembered an apple core I had set aside while driving and decided to try and pick it up. I carefully balanced my water on top of my tablet and reached down with my free hand to retrieve what was left of my apple.

Apparently, I wasn't careful enough, because a flood of water suddenly splashed into my lap and filled the seat I was still sitting in. Not only was the water ridiculously cold, but it simultaneously soiled the front and back of my pants. It literally looked as if I had just had a colossal accident.

When I telephoned my wife for moral support (and advice), she was quick to point out, "Nobody else carries an open cup of water while driving other than you, Brad." Let's assume she was right because she usually is. Most people carry water bottles instead of huge coffee mugs full of water. I get that, but it's never been a problem before. Here's where this story gets interactive.

Let's play a quick game of #ReclaimingOurCalling "What would you do?"

A.) Skip the in-service training

B.) Contact a hotel employee for help

C.) Try to dry the pants

D.) Head inside and pretend nothing happened

E.) Other: _____

I'm not sure if this will work, but I'd love for you to send me a message or picture on social media with your response (A, B, C, D, or E) before you keep reading. I'm curious how your thought process might have helped me avoid the downward spiral I'm about to share. (And to be completely honest, I'd love to share your response with my wife to prove the decision-making I'm about to unpack wasn't as bad as it might sound.) Now back to the interactive story . . .

I admit to briefly considering Option A, but skipping meetings is not my style—and this was an important training. I wasn't sure what I would even ask a hotel employee to help me with, so Option B didn't make much sense at the time either. I tried to dab the water off my pants in the parking lot, but they were so drenched, it didn't make a dent. After that, I decided to head inside and tried to act as normal as possible, so I suppose if you guessed Options C or D you're partially right.

I made my way to our meeting space and quietly checked in with a colleague to inform her I needed to take care of an issue. My colleague didn't miss a beat and suggested going to the hotel athletic club to use one of the hand dryers. This sounded like a great idea, so I swallowed my pride (again) and walked through the crowded conference center hallways pretending to be more confident than soggy.

I made it inside the hotel athletic club and did a quick scan for hand dryers. Unfortunately, the only thing I saw were things a person can't unsee. It hadn't occurred to me how busy a hotel locker room might be in the middle of the day. I presumed all the gentlemen in the athletic club were retired, and I quickly left the locker room so as to offer them the post-shower privacy they clearly needed.

As I walked out of the locker room and reassessed the situation, I realized I still had about fifteen minutes until my meeting was scheduled to start. My pants definitely needed help, and I debated asking a hotel employee if I could borrow a hair dryer, but that seemed too high maintenance. I mustered up my courage (and mental blinders) and headed back into the hotel locker room.

I proceeded to the least crowded bench in that locker room and tried to ignore all the men around me who needed towels more than I did. I pried off my cowboy boots, removed my water-laden pants, and put my boots back on. As I vigorously shook my pants in a futile attempt to air dry them, another older gentleman entered the locker room. Without missing a beat, he looked at me and quipped, "Looks like you're getting ready for a gun fight," or something to that effect.

Evidently, the sight of me in my skivvies and cowboy boots was too much for the entire room because this retired crowd started to circle the wagons while simultaneously adopting me as one of their own.

I sheepishly informed them I was trying to dry my pants before an important school meeting. Somehow, my new friends took that to mean I was giving a speech, because everyone started giving me advice on how to connect with my audience. One of them suggested I picture the audience in their underwear to level the playing field. (These guys were quick.)

It was around this same time I realized my pants were not drying as quickly as I needed them to. And besides that, I was really working up a sweat trying to shake them dry. I decided to throw my pants in the sauna for five minutes or so, hoping the intense temperature would zap the water right out of them. As I entered the sauna I was blasted by high heat and another curious (and underclothed) onlooker from inside the sauna. I quickly positioned my pants on the bench and stepped back into the locker room to cool off and wait.

That's when my new friends continued to give me public speaking advice. In an obvious hat-tip to William Shakespeare, one older gentleman suggested I start my speech by saying (insert dramatic throat-clear here) . . .

"Friends, Romans, countrymen, lend me your pants."

After a few more minutes of connecting with my locker room compatriots, I knew it was time to gather myself and get to my meeting. I collected my pants from the sauna and tried to pry my cowboy boots off—which seemed more difficult than normal to remove due to the heat and humidity in the locker room. I will admit a fleeting (and extremely ridiculous) thought crossed my mind—I may have made some new friends that day, but there was *no way* I was going to ask a partially dressed stranger to help pry off my boots.

I wriggled, hopped, sat, and wrestled each boot off while sliding along the bench. After that, I put my pants on and noticed they were still damp, but the water line definitely was less prominent. I tucked in my shirt and took a final minute to dab myself dry with a towel before saying goodbye to my new friends.

Once I was back in the conference center, I was a little sweaty but a lot less self-conscious. I shared how I had resolved my situation with my wife later that day, and she suggested I could have left my cowboy boots off while tending to things in the locker room to make less of a scene. At the same time, she knows the germophobe in me would *never* waltz around a public restroom or locker room without footwear on. The fact that I came startlingly close to reenacting a scene from my dad's horseshoe-playing days on the lake (wearing only his cowboy boots and Speedo) is not lost on me either.

Lesson Learned: The obvious lesson for me is to start carrying a water bottle. Aside from that, I do think there's an underlying lesson here. The cross-generational connections I made in that locker room reminded me of all the good in the world. I continue to think about how our schools might form more meaningful connections with people with whom we don't always interact. The older gentlemen I met that morning were supportive, engaging, and downright fun to be around.

— *Voices from the Field* —————————

Anyone who has worked in a school understands twerns happen on a regular basis. These silly stories and embarrassing moments are part of what make us human. I felt it only fitting to invite a few friends to share some final *Teaching Things That Will Remain Nameless*:

"We recently wrapped up an evening literacy event, and one of our students was serving lemonade. I stopped by to say hi and also shared how thirsty I was. He looked at me and sincerely stated, 'That's sad, Mrs. Colon, because all Happy Hours are over right now.'"

—Lynmara Colon,
director of EL Programs and Services, Virginia

"I received a report that somebody had gone to the bathroom in the sink outside the boys' bathroom. We eventually learned the culprit had first attempted to use the garbage can, but it was too tall to squat over. We took time to figure out why this had happened, and the student shared that somebody had told him a monster was hiding in the bathroom, so he was afraid to go inside. You can't make this stuff up!"

—Mark French,
principal, Minnesota

"We had a dog wander into our school. Since it belonged to an address that was only a couple blocks away, I picked it up to return it to the owners. I didn't realize the dog had a shock collar on until I carried it into its yard. The result was shocking, to say the least."

—Jay Posick,
principal, Wisconsin

"Each year, I have to teach many of the Pre-K and Kindergarten boys what the stand-up urinals are for in the bathroom. They often come out with wet backs asking, 'Where is the toilet paper?'"

—Joseph Kapuchuck,
principal, Virginia

Here is a final Easter egg shared in honor of Mrs. MacLean. Good luck!

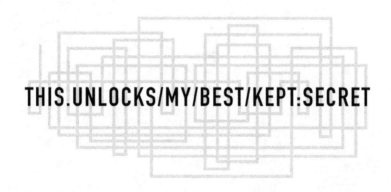

THIS.UNLOCKS/MY/BEST/KEPT:SECRET

Let's *Reclaim Our Calling* and Make Meaningful Change a Reality in *Your* Organization

Reclaiming Our Calling

What would school look like if we held the whole learner in the same regard as high-stakes test scores? This keynote is a refreshingly honest and practitioner-friendly message that will help you meet your school's goals while helping all students connect to their passions.

Let's turn off autopilot mode and set our sights on learning that lasts.

Champion Literacy, Slay Reading Logs, and BookTalk like a Wizard

If sharing the books we love is the heart of literacy, providing students time to read books they've selected is the soul. This keynote is part inspiration and part call-to-action. Learn how to create a culture of literacy and walk away with spellbinding strategies you can implement tomorrow.

Renegade Leadership

This keynote brings an inspiring blend of personal stories and humor that will change the way you think about technology leadership. Learn how to unleash student and staff potential while dismantling barriers to innovation. Collect examples of the Renegade CODE in action so you can champion meaningful change in your sphere of influence.

Inventing the Future Through Failure

Want to learn the secret to success? That's a different keynote… let's have a real conversation about failure! Empowering others requires humility, risk-taking, and honest dialogue. This keynote will reveal some of my "epic fails" and highlight some important learning that resulted. Let's delve into the difficulties we encounter when doing the real work in education.

Go to BradGustafson.com for information on speaking requests and book-study resources.

Empower

What Happens When Students Own Their Learning

By A.J. Juliani and John Spencer

In an ever-changing world, educators and parents must take a role in helping students prepare themselves for *anything*. That means unleashing their creative potential! In *Empower*, A.J. Juliani and John Spencer provide teachers, coaches, and administrators with a roadmap that will inspire innovation, authentic learning experiences, and practical ways to empower students to pursue their passions while in school.

Learner-Centered Innovation

Spark Curiosity, Ignite Passion, and Unleash Genius

By Katie Martin

Learning opportunities and teaching methods must evolve to match the ever-changing needs of today's learners. In *Learner-Centered Innovation*, Katie Martin offers insights into how to make the necessary shifts and create an environment where learners at every level are empowered to take risks in pursuit of learning and growth rather than perfection.

Unleash Talent

Bringing Out the Best in Yourself and the Learners You Serve

By Kara Knollmeyer

In *Unleash Talent*, educator and principal *Kara Knollmeyer* explains that by exploring the core elements of talent—passion, skills, and personality traits—you can uncover your gifts and help others do the same. Whether you are a teacher, administrator, or custodian, this insightful guide will empower you to use your unique talents to make a powerful impact on your school community.

About the Author

Dr. Brad Gustafson's life is defined by his faith, family, and desire to help kids—and the educators who serve them—succeed. He is a practicing principal, speaker, bestselling author, National School Boards Association "20 to Watch," Digital Innovation in Learning Award winner, and Minnesota Principal of the Year. He serves on Scholastic's Principal Advisory Board and is a national advisor with Future Ready Schools. He cohosts *UnearthED*, a popular school leadership podcast.

🌐 BradGustafson.com

🐦 @GustafsonBrad

📷 GustafsonBrad

f facebook.com/GustafsonBrad

CPSIA information can be obtained
at www.ICGtesting.com
Printed in the USA
LVHW081019070619
620511LV00018B/309/P